I ntroduction:

This is not my life story or an autobiography. I've been around for 54 years now and for the most part, it has been much like anyone else's life. In fact, it's been very boring. I will be referring to certain instances in my life where I feel they are relevant but this is the story of my time in Lindos.

Many people have written books of this sort. Everyone has a favourite place in the world, be it a bolt hole, a favourite holiday destination, or a place in which they lived which contains many happy memories.

My version is the latter, or is it a combination of the latter and its aforementioned?

Or is it just all three of them?

Lindos, on the small island of Rhodes, which forms part of the Dodecanese islands, which, if you understood the Greek language, means at least one of twelve islands. And that is my happy place.

Dhodheka is the Greek word for the number twelve and it is pronounced 'thothecka'. I've heard many tourists attempting to speak Greek which is a fantastic thing. They don't always get the pronunciation right but the wonderful thing about Greek people is they will never mock you for having a go at their language even if you make a complete mess of it. You see, many people claim to be able to speak Greek, and I know many that do, and they speak it fluently, but they still retain their local British dialect. If you want to learn to speak Greek, but you intend to travel far and wide in Greece, try mimicking the accent of a Greek newsreader for instance. If you intend to settle down on a particular island or in a particular resort, try mimicking the accent of the locals. Even on small Greek islands, the accent will change from village to village.

Rhodes is a magical island, containing many resorts varying from traditional Greek fishing villages to more commercial. Some are built for purpose and some are adapted for purpose. I would class Lindos in the latter, in that it was around for a long time before the tourists discovered it and the locals realised there could possibly be some money to be made.

Lindos was founded by the Dorians led by the King Tlepolemus of Rhodes, who arrived in about the 10th century BC. The Acropolis Of Lindos was built in the early 14th century by The Knights of St John. As I would discover and learn later, building works would regularly be halted as ancient artefacts were discovered during excavation works. It is obviously a place that has been around for many years, as you will know if you've been there, but it has been adapted to cope with its popularity as a holiday resort.

It was a place that I discovered by accident, but one that would shape my identity, cure my insecurities, and eventually define my future. I spent six seasons working and living in Lindos and, for all the troubles it brought me, the end rewards were priceless, as it has made me the person I am today.

I have many clear memories of my time there and this book intends to catalogue those memories and not to name or shame anyone who crossed my path along my journey, for whatever reason. I won't be listing or boasting about my conquests as it isn't relevant to the purpose of this book.

I wanted to put these memories down in print or in e-form for anyone who wants to read them. Maybe for future generations of my family or just for those who knew me during my time there. You may be mentioned in this book or you may not, but if you are it will be in a good light. This book is about me and all the many mistakes I made in my journey through my life in Lindos, but it is also about all those who lived there and experienced my misdemeanours and were gracious enough to give me a second chance. It is also an opportunity for those that thought they know me, well, actually......you didn't. I had a personality and was well known but I was a private person and despite my apparent outgoing personality, I would often be happier in my own company.

For that reason, I dedicate this book to each and every one of you.

If you're ready, let's read on.

Chapter One

The Preamble

It was 1990, or thereabouts. I don't really remember which month it was, but I had just met a girl. She was my first girlfriend, or my first proper girlfriend, in that she was someone who had agreed to see me again after our first night together. That's not entirely true. I had known her as *one of the lads* for about a year as she used to frequent the same bar as I did with my regular drinking mates. She would go out drinking with her older sister and they would always be present in our regular drinking haunt, which was a downstairs bar, that is to say, it was below ground floor level, in a town centre hotel in the town where I lived. Lock-ins were frequent and my mates and

I would often drink until the early hours of the morning, under the pretext that it was a hotel bar and it had a residents licence. The hotel owners didn't care as we would spend money and we were far more entertaining than the guests who stayed at the hotel.

She was a nice girl, and I fancied her so, eventually, we ended up in my bedroom, at my parents' house, where we consummated our relationship. It led to a relationship that started well but grew more fractious as time progressed.

It turned out she could drink me under the table, which, as a proud male with a salacious appetite for alcohol made me feel inadequate, and our nights out would often end in drink-fuelled arguments. I suppose I should have been grateful when it ended but I was distraught and inconsolable for weeks. Our relationship lasted for 18 months and didn't end well, and by that I mean it wasn't amicable. We have never spoken to this day and one of my last vengeful acts was to have sex with one of her best friends. I don't know if she ever found out or if her friend ever confessed to her, as sometimes happens.

I wasn't good with girls. I didn't lose my virginity at school as some of my school friends claimed to have done, and although this girlfriend wasn't my first, there wasn't a long list of conquests or relationships behind her. I was probably 18 or 19 years old before I *became a man.* You would think I would remember exactly how old I was but all I really remember was that it wasn't how I expected it to be, especially when you consider all the *videos* I had watched up to that point. I wasn't her first anyway and we never repeated that experience.

I didn't have the confidence to chat girls up and always relied on them to make the first move. That would fire my enthusiasm and often bring satisfactory end results. If a girl spoke to me and it was clear she was interested then I would find the courage to carry on with a conversation, albeit Dutch courage. My problem was, I had no starting point of conversation. I either found a girl attractive or I didn't and if I didn't I wouldn't even give her a second glance. If I did, however, I would just assume that she would be out of my league and not interested in someone who was, by my own admission, just a very ordinary-looking boy who could have done with putting some meat on his bones.

So there you have it. I'm too good for the ugly girls but not quite good enough for the pretty ones. These doubts were only what was going on in my head and perhaps I should have just targeted the ugly ones instead of trying to punch above my weight.

1992 had arrived, my longest-standing relationship was over and there was a UK recession in the offing. The country was in a bad way, and the construction industry, of which I was part, was starting to suffer. I had been part of the pre slump boom in the late eighties where work was plentiful, overtime was readily available and you could earn pretty much what you wanted to. I was young and eager and I would work all over the country, staying away in B&B accommodation, paid for by my employers, and with my overtime and out of town expenses payments I was earning upwards of £500 a week. It doesn't sound much but back then, a pint of beer cost a quid, a packet of cigarettes was about £3, and I was living at home and paying my mum housekeeping of £20 a week. Realising that a slump was on the way, I knuckled down and worked hard, stopped going out and wasting my money on drink to give myself a chance of a better life.

That all changed for me one day when I took a journey into Banbury Town Centre with the sole ambition of refreshing my wardrobe. On the spur of the moment, I stopped off into a travel agent and asked where I could fly to, very cheaply, and very quickly.

I was offered a flight to Rhodes, staying in the resort of Lindos, leaving early in the morning. It was two weeks, flight and accommodation included, for the miserly sum of £140. I paid immediately with cash and rushed home to tell my mum and dad. Mum seemed pleased and helped me pack my suitcase. Dad seemed nonplussed and unconcerned although I realise now that he was probably pleased for me.

As I boarded the Flights Bus from Banbury Bus Station to Gatwick Airport, I had no idea where I was going or how this simple journey would define my life ahead. All I knew was that I was either going on holiday or I was looking to escape abroad and work in a different country.

I arrived at Rhodes Airport in the early hours of the evening. Tourism in Greece in the 90s was huge. Four aeroplanes would arrive at Rhodes Airport from four different UK airports within minutes of each other and all of a sudden there would be nearly two thousand people searching for luggage on two antiquated conveyors which didn't display the flight numbers. This process was repeated several times a day and this was just flights from the UK. It took almost as long to get your luggage as it did to fly there and there was no such thing as air-conditioned airports back then. The process of getting your luggage back was frustrating if it even turned up. Weight limits weren't so much of a restriction so many families would arrive with suitcases full of enough clothes for a different outfit every night, not to mention a selection of foodstuffs that they thought they would be unable to get in Greece. Teabags were the obvious choice but I would learn of people who would come with a suitcase full of tinned food, completely prepared to spend their whole holiday self-catering, as many apartments were.

The transfer bus was on the long route through all the resorts on Rhodes on the way to Lindos and my first and most vivid memory of arriving on Greek soil was the sight of a young couple having sex up against a shop wall in Faliraki. For some reason, I found this appalling but I may just have been tired. At this point, I still had no idea when I would arrive in Lindos.

When I finally did, I started chatting to a few people who had been on the same transfer bus as me. The luggage transfer system in Lindos hasn't changed to this day. You unload your suitcases in the car-park at the top of the village, and a Greek man loads them onto a hybrid of a motor-ised trike and a pickup truck and takes them down to your accommodation while your travel rep escorts you through the village to said accommodation.

One of the lads on the transfer bus, Simon, if I recall, had been to Lindos before and suggested that after we had been shown to our rooms, that we all meet up in Yianni's Bar. It was clear that he had been to Lindos before as he seemed to know everyone as we followed our travel rep through the streets and was repeating the same Greek phrase to everyone he met. I don't remember that phrase, but it was probably something like *Yiasou filé or éla.*

Yiasou filé just means *hello my friend* and *éla* is just a generic word that the Greeks use for any purpose. It can mean anything from a simple reaction to a surprise visit from someone you haven't seen for a while or it could mean *WTF?*, if you add the correct gesticulations. If you say *éla edho* it just means *come here.*

Here starteth and endeth the first Greek lesson in this book. I will be testing you on this later. Or perhaps not.

I should say the accents are added for phonetic purposes and not to be confused with French. The hybrid of those two languages would be *Freek* or *Freak,* which would be a more appropriate description for Simon. That was the first and only time I ever heard him speak Greek and I must admit after a few days of knowing him, I deduced that he was a bit of a dick and managed to disassociate myself from him.

This wasn't the real issue though because, as I dropped my suitcase and ghetto blaster that I had bought at Gatwick Duty-Free, into my room and made my way back through the winding maze that is Lindos, it was raining, and I mean actually pissing down. Having arrived in the dark and staying at the far end of the village, my route back to Yianni's Bar turned out to be more complicated than I expected and I eventually found my bearings – and Yianni's Bar – after having walked past it at least five times. I was soaking wet but I was here and I was more than ready for a beer.

The rain didn't stop for four days. This was early May, 1992. I had come here for the weather and it didn't seem to be happening.

When the rain finally stopped, the last ten days of the holiday were glorious. I got a healthy all-over tan without getting sunburnt as I had done the last time I had ventured outside the English shores in 1988 when I'd had an alcohol-fuelled holiday with a few mates in Lanzarote.

At that time in my life, this holiday was everything I needed, but the ghetto blaster I had bought at the duty-free shop at Gatwick Airport had turned out to be faulty. I'd got back to my apartment after my first night out and decided to play one of the many cassette tapes that I'd brought with me. It transpired that one of the speakers wasn't working. I knew I could probably fix it but I didn't have any tools with me.

I sat in my apartment for the next four days listening to the rain crash down outside and listening to my mixtapes through one speaker.

Frustratingly, it would only rain in the day-time which was supposed to be beach time. From the balcony of my apartment, I could see a beach that was within spitting distance. It appeared to be down a very steep hill but then again I was only 26 years old, fit and healthy and even though the descent would be easy, I couldn't imagine that the ascent at the end of the day would have served me any problems.

When the weather finally cleared and the rain disappeared I packed my beach gear together and made my first visit to the beach.

At the bottom of the hill was a smallish beach with sunbeds and the rear of the beach was adorned with various beach restaurants and fast food outlets. I was drawn, almost magnetically, to an establishment with an English name.

The Sunburnt Arms.

As the man I perceived to be the owner took my breakfast order, I realised he was as English as I was. I didn't know at this stage that I would forge a relationship with him and his family that still exists to this day.

As he came out to take my empty plate, I casually asked if he had a screwdriver I could borrow and explained my reasons for wanting to dismantle my ghetto blaster. His short retort was "only if you bring it down here. I don't lend my tools out to anyone".

I complied with his request and brought it down the following day and sat on a table at the side and proceeded to investigate the fault. I'm sorry to say I never really discovered why it didn't work and I got a full refund at the duty-free shop I had bought it from.

Was this the best part of my holiday?

No. I'd gone looking to possibly find work but prepared to at least have a holiday. As I was walking through Lindos one afternoon, I passed a building site that I hadn't previously spotted. A lone male was working on this site who, from outside appearances, didn't appear to be a local. As Martin and I introduced ourselves to each other it turned out that we were only geographically about 20 miles apart back home. I asked if there were "any jobs going", and before I knew it, Martin, myself and another English lad were loading rocks that had been dumped at the top of the village into a smaller vehicle that could navigate itself freely through the narrow streets of Lindos. It was around 3 pm and the sun was burning and the sheer physical exertion of handling rocks was cutting my hands open with every action. I had spent my working life in the UK in the construction industry but I soon realised that it was an entirely different situation here.

We finished our task, got paid fairly well for our efforts and went to have a drink in *Jody's Flat.* This was an English owned bar and it was the only English bar in the village or the only one that I knew of anyway. It seemed to be where all the English workers would congregate and there seemed to be a lot of them.

Was this the best thing that happened to me on my holiday?

No. Of course not. I met a girl. This is a bit tortuous but I was having a quiet drink with Martin when he spotted a girl that he knew from back home, from the same town as him. She was on holiday with a few friends, one of which was her ex-husband and they were staying at an underdeveloped resort a few kilometres north of Lindos. As we were all geographically close, I latched onto their group and had just some of the most fun drunken nights with them.

I really liked her and towards the end of the holiday, I had managed to woo her somehow and I took her back to my room where we had sex, and again the night after. When you are in your twenties, having sex with a girl more than once is enough to constitute or justify entering into a relationship with them. I made up my mind, just in time that I had found myself a new girlfriend and I would be travelling back home on my return flight.

We seemed to get on and so we agreed to carry on our relationship when we got back home. It seemed like my holiday plan had worked. I could finally move on from the break-up of my last relationship, and at least I wouldn't have to travel all over the UK to see her. It was like having a girlfriend at a safe distance.

This is when my lack of experience with girls reared its ugly head again. I thought at that innocent time in my life that if you had a girlfriend, you could just go out drinking with your mates and call on your girlfriend for sex when it suited you.

This happened a few times when we got back home, even to the point that she would turn up at my parents' house in the evening and I would get home from the pub after drinking with my mates, most probably drunk, and she would be waiting to whisk me off in her car back to her flat to have sex. It carried on for a few months like this until she decided that I wasn't committed enough and I was dumped.

Again.

This set me right back to the position I had been in just a few months before and I decided in my now very outdated opinion, that women only existed on this earth for having sex with and nothing else. I'd failed myself once more.

I made a decision to do something about this, and after I'd cried about it down the pub with my mates, who didn't seem to care, I needed to make an immediate plan. I had made some good friends in my short two weeks abroad and I felt there was more to come. I'd fallen in love with Lindos and everything I thought it could offer me whether it be short term or long term.

Are you ready? Let's read on.

Chapter Two

Season One: The First Summer

I had been back in the UK for a couple of months and was starting to get restless. I had a game plan in mind but didn't know how to execute it, or more to the point, I had no money behind me. I had found a job with a local firm that involved nothing more exciting than wiring up electrical control boxes for export to local and international industries. I enjoyed the work as, with an electrical apprenticeship already behind me, it meant that I could do this job with my eyes closed. I'd saved about £500 in spending money and a little more in reserve to afford flights etcetera, for a second stab at finding a life abroad in the sun. We were a small team of about ten blokes and we got on really well at work. Radio One was playing in the workshop and the buzz of activity was often drowned out by the sound of ten blokes singing, very badly, at the tops of their voices.

I knew that my time there would be short-lived and it was only about earning enough money to build some cash reserves to go and have another shot at life abroad. I finished work there on a Friday, and never went back. I had only been there about six weeks in total.

I'd honestly intended to tell my parents about my intentions but they had disappeared on one of their foreign holidays, as they often did without notice. They had three grownup kids still living at home at that time and felt they could leave at a moments notice and trust us to look after their house.

I seized my chance.

I booked a flight back to Rhodes and then went home and packed the biggest suitcase I could find with everything I thought I might need for an extended break. The repercussions of that act would come later.

Before I left the first time around Martin had given me an address where I could find him if I ever came back. That address turned out to be useless as he moved on shortly afterwards but it would prove useful in the future. He probably didn't expect me to ever turn up so when I did he was gobsmacked. He had moved on from his previous accommodation and had found a cheap room which he shared with the other "rock shifting operative" that I had previously worked with, if only for one day.

Martin introduced me to the "landlord" of this accommodation who will be forever known as SuperJock. I was informed that there were no rooms left but I could always sleep on the roof, for free, if I needed to.

And so there I was, sleeping on a roof for a couple of weeks, most probably in full view of all the rooftop restaurant diners but I didn't care as it was a start at least. Besides anything else, it was August and the daytime temperatures were pushing 40 degrees and it never dipped much below 30 at night. I had had my own personal aircon, something of a luxury in the 90s.

After a couple of days, I decided to go in search of some work. I was financially able to withstand about a month without working but that wasn't my intention.

By word of mouth, I learned that there was a local man that needed a big hole dug in his back garden to allow the installation of a cesspit.

I was introduced to him and was given simple instructions. There were four pieces of wood stuck in the ground, perpendicular to each other. He handed me a shovel.

"*You make hole here, two metres down*", he said pointing to the sticks. "*When you finished, I pay you. Come tomorrow early before the sun is in the sky*".

I duly arrived at about 6 am the following day and proceeded to dig. It wasn't long before the sun showed its head over the horizon and things started to warm up very quickly. I was already getting agitated but to add to my agitation a lot of buzzy insects, possibly bees, maybe wasps, but most likely hornets were starting to congregate around my work area. I was only about a metre deep by this time and I'd had enough. This man lived just off the beach and his back garden was entirely sand. As much as I shovelled, the sand kept falling back into the hole.

This wasn't what I came here to do. I threw my shovel down and went back to my *apartment*. I had a shower and continued to scour the village for Sits Vac. I went back the following day to apologise for my poor efforts only to be told that he had already booked a plumber to come from Rhodes town and because the cesspit wasn't ready he had to pay the plumber 5000 drachmas as a cancellation fee and I wouldn't be paid as a result.

In my world, you never book a tradesman to come and carry out a job until the preparation has been done. I took the wage loss on the chin and learnt something new that day but I would get revenge later on that year.

I'd started to get to know some of the English who were working there. Those who had come to do the same as I had, to spend a summer in the sun.

I was told that there was a bar looking for *Staff.* I found the bar *Tres Lobos* and was given the job as a drinks waiter. I'd never done anything like that in my life although

I had worked behind the bar in a couple of pubs in the UK. It seemed easy enough and I figured I would be meeting people, or girls, more to the point.

I'd been doing the job for about a week and seemed to be coping with it and the young-ish man who I had thought was the boss was happy. His English was adequate and we would sit, chat, and drink at the bar together in the quiet periods. It was about the sixth night when a woman came in, who was actually the boss/owner. She told me that I wasn't holding the drinks tray properly and I should carry it in the way that professional waiters do. I took a drinks order from a group of five girls and took it to the bar.

She loaded the drinks onto the tray which were all cocktails and probably quite expensive. As I cautiously carried the tray back to the girls with the tray perched on the flat of my palm I had a sense that things were going to go disastrously wrong. I took the first drink which was nearest to me, and the whole centre of gravity of the tray changed, sending it toppling towards them and covering them with their drinks. It was early evening and they had all dressed up for the night ahead.

I couldn't think of anything useful to say so I just held up the one drink I had taken off the tray and asked sheepishly, "which one of you ordered this?". I didn't get a reply, just a lot of stunned looks, so I just placed the drink down and left the bar and never went back.

I felt good though. I'd been getting paid daily so I wasn't owed anything apart from my partial shift that evening, and I had about 30,000 drachmas on top of what I'd bought with me and I was living rent-free, albeit on a roof. I was conserving the money I had and was trying to limit my alcohol intake and daily cigarette usage.

I thought it was about time I tried to contact my mother. Mobile phones weren't a thing back then and it would be a couple more years until we would see telephone kiosks being installed around Lindos that were operated by telephone cards that could be bought from supermarkets.

The only option was to use the antiquated phone systems in the local money exchange bureaus but they were hopeless and it was impossible to make a call anywhere outside of Greece. I decided to put pen to paper and I wrote home, explaining where I was and why. When the reply finally came – the postal system was slow – I could sense the disappointment and upset I had caused my mum. She had not been happy at the way I had decided to up sticks and leave, especially as I had unfinished income tax affairs outstanding. It wasn't a huge amount, a couple of thousand pounds and no more, but she was having to deal with it and return any red letters with *Unknown at this address* scrawled across the envelope.

She knew exactly where I was and I would thank her later for trying to protect me.

So life was good. My circle of friends was building and I felt happier than I had done in a long time, and then the bombshell dropped. Superjock explained that I could no longer sleep on the roof as the owner of the villa was back in town for a couple of days. I needed to find something quickly and the best I could do was rent tourist accommodation but it was expensive at 5000 drachmas a night for a twin room with shared bathroom facilities. I managed to find another worker who needed a room so we shared the cost.

I suppose it would be beneficial to the reader at this point about the situation I was in. 2500 drachmas were worth about £7:50 in sterling, which is not an unreasonable room rate per night but when you consider that would be half of your daily wages and then you need to think about how much money you will have left after you've paid your rent and how much you'll have left to eat or survive. Life in Lindos was on a day to day basis, a very hand to mouth existence.

I was still unemployed though. I heard of a job going at one of the village restaurants as a washer upper. The wages were ok. It promised just a couple of hours of work after the restaurant closed in the evening. I felt it would pay me enough to cover my rent and some more while I carried on looking for something more suitable. I turned up on the first night and went into this tiny room at the back of the restaurant which contained a sink and more plates, cutlery and pots and pans than I had ever seen in one place at any time in my life. It was as though they never cleaned up as they went along and just replaced the dirty stuff with new stuff. The crockery and cutlery were relatively easy but the pots and pans had stuff burnt into them and I was trying to wash this stuff up in cold water and detergent. The room was airless and hot and it would still have been at least 30 degrees in there. I managed to last about an hour before I excused myself on the pretence of going to the toilet. I left through the first exit I could find and as I breathed in the relative coolness of the night air I started to wonder if I would ever find a job here that I could be happy with.

I stopped off at *Niko's Bar* on my way back to my room. It was a bar that I had found whilst I had been on holiday and I quite liked it there. The DJ was a bit more thoughtful than some of the other DJs in the village and I liked the music that he played. After a couple of drinks, I decided to turn it in and make the short walk to my room. Before I even put the key in the lock, it was apparent that my roommate Ben had found himself company for the night. What surprised me most was that anyone would dare to enter that room for any reason.

Ben used to kick off his trainers in the room when he got back and, owing partly to the fact that he didn't wear socks, the smell was horrendous. It used to take an age for the pathetic fan that we had in there to finally dismiss the smell through the open window.

On that particular night, I decided to sleep on a plastic chair in the courtyard. In fairness to Ben, but not to excuse him for his poor foot hygiene, he could get the girls. He was a good looking lad and he had the chat techniques, and these were two qualities that I lacked. As his conquest left in the morning, I pretended to still be asleep but I opened one eye as she opened the door and walked along the courtyard to the villa gates and I had to admire his choice and his standards.

But really, things were starting to get serious. I had no job and I'd already walked out of two jobs losing me a potential three to four nights rent money. The return flight that I had come out on had already left without me and I was *stranded* for want of a better description. I took an early shower and walked down to the beach. I had hardly used The Sunburnt Arms on my second visit to Lindos, save for the occasional bacon butty for breakfast as I was trying to conserve funds, but I reckoned that Cliff, the owner, would have his ears on the ground as to where they may be possible job vacancies.

It was a good and productive move. I had failed to spot that the restaurant next door, named simply as Pallas Taverna, was also owned/rented by an English couple. I suppose I had just assumed, from the name, that it would be Greek-owned. I learned that they were looking for a waiter. I reckoned that they would excuse my lack of ability to correctly hold a tray and went next door to enquire.

The Sunburnt Arms and Pallas Taverna were two very different establishments. If I recall correctly, they were not in direct competition with each other despite being English owned and had agreed to offer different menus outside of the usual breakfast standards.

I went next door and met Brigid. She was delightfully tall and pretty with short-cropped reddish hair. She was softly spoken and friendly and I was immediately hired. I got to meet the assistant chef Carolyn and the two other waiters, Carl, a young straggly haired boy and Bob. Bizarrely, I had already met Bob earlier on in the year when I had been on holiday so was surprised to see him still there and working as he was on holiday himself at the time.

We made a great team. Carl had done waiting duties back in the UK and it was clear he knew what he was doing as he could carry a huge tray upstairs to the rooftop area with one outstretched palm. I would later learn that you sort of balance it on your forearm as well and Carl would often criticise me for my lack of waiter skills but I didn't care. I just used to carry the tray with both hands and perch it on the edge of the table as I delivered the individual plates. Carl was the dancing waiter. He would dance through the kitchen in time to the many cassette tapes we had, as he took the orders out to the tables. Bob was the singing waiter. He would sing along to the cassette tapes and I was impressed with his voice and vocal range. Me? I'm a drummer. I just hit things in time but have no other musical ability and I certainly can't dance. Or sing. Or carry a tray properly, but this is a beach restaurant serving English grub, and none of our customers really care that much.

We had regular customers for two weeks at a time and I would make it my business to get to know their names and their favourite tipples or even how they liked their breakfast tea or coffee – strong, weak, or indifferent. My confidence with people in general, but more importantly, the female of the species, was growing and I felt comfortable in making the first move for the first time in my life. Finally, I felt confident in chatting up girls, and I wouldn't get upset or dejected at a rebuff.

The most memorable incident of my time at Pallas Taverna was when Carolyn handed me a plate of something or other with chips to be taken upstairs to the rooftop area. It was somewhere between breakfast and lunchtime and I had started to get hungry. I stole a chip from the plate to temporarily sate my appetite before carrying the tray of food upstairs. What I had forgotten was that there was a small window on the rooftop terrace which gave a clear view of the kitchen and my chip thieving. As I placed the plates of food down in front of the customers the gentleman of the party replied with a "Thank you", and a pause. "Would you like any more of my chips?", he enquired. I felt myself disappearing through the floor of the rooftop area and expected – and hoped – that the ground below would swallow me up. I walked down the stairs with my empty tray and explained my predicament.

Bob, ever the one to come up with a solution took a saucer from the crockery pile and placed a solitary chip on it. "Take this upstairs", he suggested. Full of confidence, I placed the saucer with the solitary chip on a tray and made the walk upstairs.

"Apologies Sir", I started. "Here is your

missing chip".

I received a wry smile in return and went back to carry on with my duties. After half an hour so, I saw the family descend the stairs and return to the beach with a cheery wave. I assumed I'd been forgiven for my earlier misdemeanour so I went upstairs to clear the table. On the saucer that had contained the solitary chip was a 1000 drachma note, left as a tip, but placed on top of the note was "that" chip.

It was not long after this that I met Brigid's husband Chris. I found him to be a strange character. Knowing what I know now, he was probably the worst case of OCD I have ever met and he most likely had ADHD. He would come down to the restaurant and start frantically scrubbing surfaces down as he thought they were *greasy*. When you have a beach restaurant where customers regularly come inside the waiting area laden with suntan oils and SPF 50 lathered in, it's not unreasonable to assume that they may transmit some of those *oils* to the surfaces. I gelled with him however and I explained my predicament that I was essentially paying out almost as much in rent as I was earning.

What I didn't know either, was that he also had a bar in the village in the evening, The 60s Bar, which he joint-owned/rented with another Englishman called Chris. I had walked by this bar many times as I'd preferred the environment of The Lindian House, Manolis Bar, Socrates Bar, Il Sogno and Jody's Flat. He told me that he needed a barman for the 60s Bar.

It was the first time I had met him so I was surprised to learn that he had rented a villa for the season for his workers and there was a room available and it was rent-free.

I could have taken this room for myself but I felt a sense of obligation towards Ben and his stinking trainers and I didn't want to leave him to pay the full rent for the room so I invited him to join me. Besides anything else, I had learned that his dad also ran a restaurant in the village and that his father Keith, and Cliff, were friends. How ironic that the restaurant his father owned was the one I had walked out of after being confronted with piles of washing up?

Time is a great healer but every time I catch the smell of trainers worn without socks I am transported back to those rooms, so I can't forgive, especially as Ben would continue to bring back girls and force me out to the courtyard for the night. At least I had the decency to invite myself back to the holiday accommodation of any conquests, where the condition of the rooms would be infinitely better. Our shared room was airless and hot, and it had no fan and it was murderous to sleep in.

At last, I'm sorted. I have two jobs. It was

hard work but I got three meals a day with unlimited drinks and then I'm working in the evening in a bar with unlimited drinks. And I have free accommodation! The money pot started to refresh itself and my confidence was growing by the day.

Was this the best season of my six? I'm not sure but as October ended I came to realise that things would be closing down soon. It all came to an abrupt halt and it was akin to taking a ball from a puppy when you think it's about time he went to sleep but as you put him to bed you realise he is still excited and just needs a few more minutes to get his yah yah's out. This was me at the end of the 1992 season. It had gone by in an instant, and I was ready for so much more.

C hapter Three

Season One: A Winter Beckons

At this point, I had no idea what was in store for me. I knew it would cool down significantly from what I had been used to but I wasn't prepared for how cold the nights would be. All I knew was that I wanted to stay for the winter and I wanted to experience life in Lindos out of season.

I hadn't seen much of Martin during the summer as we had different jobs and different working schedules although I had occasionally bumped into him on a night out. I learned he was intending to stay for the winter, as was Carl, and another English boy who went by the name of Lee. I knew little of Lee, other than he had worked in a restaurant in the village as a waiter.

All of a sudden though, four English boys were planning an unprecedented stay in a foreign country and we needed somewhere to live. Our respective summer accommodation had expired, thankfully, as no accommodation that is let to workers is generally fit for habitation other than by desperate English workers.

We found some apartments at the top of the village that belonged to a local bar owner. The attraction of these apartments was that the rent was low, and by that, I mean really low. We were quoted a figure for the entire six month winter season which equated to the same as what we had been individually paying per month in the summer so it was a no brainer in that respect. On reflection, they were pretty poor but we did have separate rooms at least, and they were on such a high level that we could almost see the upper flagstones of the Acropolis of Lindos from our balcony. I'm pretty sure our oxygen levels were seriously depleted at such an altitude. This would probably be the reason we would head down into the village of an evening just to take in some normal air.

It was either that or the fact that bar prices seemed to be about fifty percent lower than what we had been used to.

There weren't many bars that had chosen to stay open for the winter but one of the ones that did was generally populated by English and a few Greeks. It had a pool table and so it felt as close to home as we could expect. We spent many a night in there enjoying the reduced price drinks menu, although I would have to say that it was more the fact that we couldn't believe how cheap it was to drink in the winter and we abused that privilege by just getting wasted most nights.

On one of these famous nights out, we had been making our way up to the upper-most summit of the village when we spied a building site. In our drunken states, we thought it would be a good idea to misap-propriate some bricks and some sand and cement mortar and build ourselves a roof-top barbecue, to which we would invite everyone that we knew who was English.

There was us four, another English girl and her Greek boyfriend, an American girl who was the housekeeper/nanny for Dave Gil-mour of Pink Floyd fame who owned or rented a villa in Lindos. There was also another English couple who were building an apartment in Gennadi, a resort further south of Lindos, and, at that point, largely underdeveloped.

They lived just downstairs from us in a villa that was owned by our very same landlord. We invited them to the barbecue as they seemed like a nice couple. It was very much a bring your own food and alcohol sort of affair but we successfully managed to cook everything without giving any of our guests food poisoning.

It was bloody cold though, despite being only just into November. I hadn't brought that many winter clothes with me so I just relied on lots of layers to keep me warm in the evenings.

Christmas was approaching and I decided it might be a good time to head back to the UK to spend a bit of time with my family. Martin and Carl had already gone back home for a brief visit leaving just Lee and myself. I had overlooked one small problem though in that not being a frequent traveller I hadn't bothered to check my passport before travelling out earlier in the year. To my horror, I realised my passport had expired and I was stranded. Knowing nothing of the protocols of renewing a passport whilst being in a foreign country or the fact that I should even be there on an extended visit I decided to call home and explain my predicament. In the winter, the phone lines were a lot less congested and calling home was more successful.

Mum came up with a solution and I don't even know if it was legal. She managed to renew my passport by post, possibly by forging my signature and she hand-delivered it to me. Yes. Instead of me having to travel home for Christmas, mum and dad came out to see me, accompanied by my brother.

I did explain to her that the weather wouldn't be that favourable and there were no charter flights but I found accommodation for them at Martins first digs. It wasn't really a tourist accommodation and the rooms weren't built for the winter so my mum went out somewhere and bought an electric bar heater and installed it into their room so that they could sleep warm at night. It was naturally passed on to me when they left.

I inherited this heater and with my electrical expertise, I bypassed the electric meter in my winter accommodation so that no one would ever have to pay for its usage.

Apart from the Greek Energy Company of course.

The landlady of the accommodation was a Mrs Effrosini, a lovely old Greek lady who would recognise me on my subsequent returns until she eventually went blind. I can't be sure, but I would surmise that she has possibly passed away by now. My mum renamed her Mrs Frosty, mainly due to the general temperature of her winter apartments.

The greatest thing about my parents' visit was that my mum could produce a first-class meal with ingredients sourced from the local supermarket and it was all prepared and cooked on two electric rings. I hadn't eaten like this in a long time and I felt like a King. I missed my mum's home cooking but I wasn't ready to return to the UK for good just yet. I felt there was an exciting season ahead and I was prepared to take it with open arms.

Martin and Carl returned ready for another season and I decided to make the trip home in early January for a couple of weeks, mainly to bring a few more clothes out and to better prepare myself for the season ahead. There were no direct flights from Rhodes to the UK in the off season so the only two options were to take an internal flight from Rhodes to Athens and then from Athens to the UK or to travel to Athens on the overnight ferry and then take the flight to the UK. The ferry trip was long and tortuous and it would mean sleeping in a chair on the lower decks but it was significantly cheaper than an internal flight and I didn't have a lot of money left so my options were limited. What little money I had needed to be preserved for my return.

As I waited for the ferry at Mandraki Harbour in Rhodes Town, my luck was about to change. Waiting in the queue was a Greek couple that I knew of who owned a restaurant in Lindos and the English couple who were building their house in Gennadi. The Greek couple were travelling to Athens but the male half had a phobia of flying and both he and his wife had taken the ferry instead, and the English couple had booked two cabins on the ferry. One for themselves and one for a friend of theirs who had come out to assist them with their building project.

The upshot of all this was I spent the evening in the first-class bar with my Greek friends instead of being in cabin class, and there was a spare bed for me to get my head down at the end of the night. The crossing was *choppy,* as they say in nautical terms, and it was the first time in my life I had ever slept overnight on a boat

The visit home was worthwhile. I managed to catch up with a few friends and I picked up a bit of work as well so I managed to top up my finances. When I returned, the apartments that we had rented had started to become a problem. They were not winter apartments and the roof would leak when it rained. There would frequently be water running down the walls. Another issue was that the thermostat on the water heater was broken and if left on for long periods, the water would boil to 100 degrees and then the pressure relief valve would burst, flooding the apartment with boiling water.

We complained to our landlord about the constant flooding of the upstairs apartments.

"It's no problem boys", he replied. "The people downstairs have gone home for the winter. You can move in, there is enough room for four people."

And so it was. Me and Lee are in one twin room and Martin is on his own in another twin room. And I'll never know how he blagged this but Carl managed to commandeer the upstairs bedroom on the mezzanine, overlooking the whole of the ground floor.

The whole building was sparse and devoid of any home comforts. Cooking facilities were rudimentary. We had a kitchen but it was outside in the courtyard. It was so cold at night that we would just light a fire in the fireplace to warm the room up and then drink beer until we were ready to go back to our rooms, normally dressed in our day clothes, and a few blankets on top.

We had no TV but we did have a radio cassette player so we could at least listen to music.

A lad named Gary who had been working in Lindos the previous year came back at this point. We all knew him, sort of, so we let him come and join us in the villa and he moved into Martin's room. The English couple had also returned but were now living elsewhere and Gary had ended up working for them, or just labouring on their building site. I don't know the precise chain of events but as I understand, Gary was getting a bit pissed off with having to do all the labouring himself while this couple and their mate watched. He complained about the situation and told them he needed another labourer to help him. I realise now that Gary was something of a lazy cunt who had no idea what hard work was. The end result of his demands was that they chucked him out of the car on their way back home, which was a Porsche something or other and told him to walk home, which was a fair few kilometres.

As they chucked him out and started to drive off, Gary swung his leg and connected his boot with the rear quarter panel of the Porsche. They didn't stop and drove on to leave him to walk home. I remember Gary bragging about his bravado act but we had no idea at that point of the repercussions that would come.

Some weeks had passed, and we had all been out for a drink one night and had probably taken far too much on board. This was a reasonably normal night for us but tonight would change everything. As we got back to the villa and retired to our respective rooms/beds we settled down for the night. A few hours later, Lee and myself were awakened from our beds to the sounds of something extremely violent taking place. The male half of the couple and his friend who was an ex-marine still had keys to the villa and had let themselves in. They were seeking revenge for the dropkick on the Porsche and Lee and I could only listen in horror as we heard the screams of Gary getting the shit beaten out of him.

Lee and I got out of our beds to investigate what was happening and we were met with the sight of an extremely large man stood at the door of Martin and Gary's room with his arms folded.

"Get back to your beds", was all he said, and we complied. I don't mind admitting that myself, and most likely Lee, were scared shitless.

The sad thing is Martin got caught in the crossfire and took a few blows himself.

In shock, we collectively agreed to report the assault to the local police which turned out to be a mistake as we subsequently became targets of investigation for any suspicious behaviour. I wasn't arrested at the time but I clearly recall Martin's experience.

The Police had travelled to Gennadi and arrested the two perpetrators. Martin and Gary were already present at the Police station as they had been arrested under suspicion so when the Police brought back the main suspects and confronted them with the accusations, they denied any involvement. The problem, and one that would be a damning indictment in the affray that had occurred that night, was that one of them had lost his wristwatch, and the Police had picked it up at the scene. When the Chief of Police questioned why the wristwatch had been found and to whom it belonged, there was no defence to present.

In our country, you would have been given the benefit of doubt of course but the judicial system in Greece lacked patience or tolerance, so the Chief of Police and his thug sidekick decided not to pursue the investigation any further but to administer their own justice.

Martin and Gary watched with horror as their two protagonists had the shit kicked out of them mercilessly by the Chief of Police and his assistant, wondering if they would be next. Thankfully that didn't happen and they were free to leave. I'm not sure if they ever came back to finish their building project but I certainly never set eyes on them again. Gary went home shortly afterwards, never to return, thankfully.

This incident made it difficult for all of us as we were now constantly under the scrutiny of The Police. In truth, neither of us should have been there without official work and health papers so we all decided to go to Rhodes Hospital for a medical and then get our work permits signed off by The Chief. I'm sure he didn't want us there but we were legal now, and consequently, he would be powerless to evict us as long as we behaved ourselves.

We became known as The Lost Boys, after the film of the same name starring Kiefer Sutherland, Corey Haim, Corey Feldman and so many others. We had no connection with the storyline of the film but it seemed appropriate to tag us thus. We were properly lost, all of us. We had little in the way of jobs or prospects or money, and we would whore ourselves around the village tagging on to whatever free barbeque was going, not to mention the prospect of a bit of free booze, whether it was a sneaky slug from an open bottle of Ouzo or Metaxa.

It wasn't an ideal existence but it kept us alive and fed.

Martin resumed his work on the building site that he had been working on in the summer and somehow, I managed to get a job, but the work was poor. Manolis, the owner and instigator of this project was trying to build and open up a nightclub in the heart of Lindos and he wanted to include a rooftop swimming pool as a bonus. Quite how he would get past the heritage laws would be a mystery but he managed to do so, probably by paying off anyone who opposed him.

He had this bizarre idea that he could make the frontage of his building in keeping with the traditional village look so he had employed a carpenter to make him some wooden moulds, most probably at great expense. We would have to coat these wooden moulds with wax and then pour a mixture of concrete and coloured sand so that he could make his own authentic looking keystones which would surround the arched doorways.

I would say that the major setback to this operation was firstly that he didn't have a clue what he was doing but more importantly, the four men he had employed to make these fake keystones had even less of a clue. That was Martin, me, an old fella called Joe, who had turned up in the winter with his wife and, I think, a twenty-ish daughter who had a boyfriend who would soon follow. I think they had only been around for a week or so before most of the young Greek lads in the village had claimed they had slept with her. In their dreams of course.

And then there was Phil.

If you are reading this Phil, you are one of the funniest, intellectual and laid back Greek people I have ever met. You have a glorious English sense of humour to boot and you were instrumental in helping me to learn the complex Greek language which, for the most part, I retain to this day.

I remember walking past Manolis' establishment that he had built one day after it had been completed and I could see that his keystones had been fixed around the door arches by the use of a rawlpug and a posidrive screw. These keystones were supposed to be cemented in but either he had used a weak mix or cement or the fact that he had no clue what he was doing meant that they soon started falling off in the slightest breeze.

If Iktinos, the architect who had been responsible for many historic Greek structures dating back to the 5th Century BC could have witnessed it he would be turning in his grave.

Martin had managed to secure himself some more suitable accommodation and if I recall, Phil was living just around the corner somewhere. Martin gave me some temporary accommodation but Phil would often be a guest in our house in the evening. He was an excellent and patient tutor.

He gave me a basic insight into the Greek language and taught me a lot of verbs and prepositions. It's not as complicated as you think. Greek is an ancient language and hasn't evolved too much over the centuries apart from the street slang and colloquialisms and many verbs form the same pattern. The verb itself is all one word. The action of the verb forms the first part of the word and the possession forms the second part.

So, just for simplicity, and phonetically....

Ti kaneis = how are you?

Ti kanoume = how are we?

Most tourists will know with a degree of inaccuracy and pronunciation that the Greek word for Thank You is *efkharisto* but if you wanted to thank someone on behalf of a group of people you belonged to, you would say *efkharistoume* which just means the possession has changed, meaning we thank you.

It would have been around this time that I met Jack properly. I had bumped into him on previous occasions in my initial holiday so he knew of me. At that time he was still working at his mum's beach restaurant. One of the main attractions for visiting day-trippers to Lindos was the Acropolis of Lindos. It was a very steep walk up the hill though so many lazy and unfit tourists would choose to hitch a ride on a donkey. I had walked the donkey track many times in my short life in Lindos and about half-way along that route was a stinking mess of wasteland which would have rubbish bags and all manner of detritus thrown into it. I came to understand that the land belonged to him and he was intending to build a bar on the footprint of the site. Carl and myself were employed and I'm pretty sure Lee was there but there was also a Belgian guy called Roland who had been a chef or a waiter somewhere in the season that had just passed. That was hard work as well. We were breaking up rocks and earth so that some sort of foundations could be built or at least Jack would have a beer cellar or some sort of underground storage. I would meet Roland again, but in a different country and another year, and I would end up working for Jack, in the bar that Jack built, with help of his father, Apostolis.

We all managed to keep ourselves going during the winter somehow but it was mainly building work or more specifically labouring.

I'm going to level with you here. I had a trade back in the UK, which was a well-respected and well-paid trade and a lot of the jobs I was employed to do in Lindos I felt were beneath me. I hated the fact that I was being given a labouring job by a nation that was centuries behind evolution in terms of building practices. Many jobs involved nothing more than shovelling piles of stuff from one location to another for no apparent purpose. The problem was, and although I never researched this properly, I feel quite confident in stating that the shovels we were supplied with were also used in the construction of the Acropolis, many centuries before. Greek tools didn't have the finesse of the tools I had been used to working with at home and although it might have had something to do with the fact that the skin on my hands had possibly softened up over the previous summer, every tool that we were ever supplied with just used to cut our hands open.

Lee and myself were contracted out to do a little job for a local man but it was just outside of Lindos in Vlicha. We were dropped off on a building site one morning and our task for the day was to use a couple of prehistoric Greek claw hammers to remove all the nails from the shuttering planks that had been used in the initial concrete forming process. We were also instructed to sort the planks into piles according to length. The problem was it was ridiculously cold and I was most likely fighting a hangover. We were promised 5000 drachmas each for our work. I don't think we had been there for much more than an hour when I decided that this wasn't a job worth getting out of bed for. I suggested to Lee that we take the thirty minute walk back to Lindos and I would sort out payments that evening. We downed tools and left.

I went back to the house of the person who had originally asked us to do this work. He wasn't at home but his English wife was. I explained that we hadn't been able to completely finish the job but we would be back tomorrow...but in the meantime...could we get paid please as we were struggling to pay our rent? She took pity on us I'm sure as we were of the same nationality and she searched around the house gathering up all the small change she could find until she had the full 10,000 drachmas to pay us.

We left with the coins jangling in our pockets and weighing our trousers down before we headed off to Remejjo's Pool Bar for a drink with our earnings.

We never went back the following day as we had promised to because the man who had hired us was the very same person who had hired me six months earlier to dig his cesspit. I don't really class this as revenge but more as a readjustment in terms of respect, but it felt good at the time. I'm happy to say that Mikhalis and I overcame our differences and we still are friends whenever I revisit Lindos.

It would have been about this time that I met Dimitris Takis and his brother in law Euripides. So the Greek tradition dictates, when a man's daughter gets married, he has to buy or build her a house to live in with her new husband. Although Euripides is a Greek name it was not so common in Lindos. Most Greek males in Lindos were either Yianni, Manolis, Giorgos, Savvas, Dimitris or Apostolis.

Euripides, historically, was a tragedian of classical Athens, but the Euripides that I knew was better known as Evripides or just Rip for short. The Rip that I knew was hardly a tragedian, but he was the proprietor and owner of what is still one of the longest standing restaurants in Lindos.

Dimitris Takis was a larger than life character with a genuine heart of gold. He was seriously overweight but he had the strength of an ox. He could pick up a 25kg bag of cement with one arm and lift it above his head as though it were a packet of cigarettes.

His father and he would run a boat trip from The Pallas beach and such was their genuity and love of the English tourists and workers alike, they would often host free boat trips for the English workers.

Captain Takis was the father of Dimitris and Kiki, to whom Evripides was married. Although he owned the house where his son, daughter and wife lived, he had separated from his wife some years before and didn't live there anymore. It was an old Greek villa with *khokaklia* pebbled flooring throughout and was typical in its appearance in that it would have a central arched doorway with an entrance courtyard and rooms to each side. Typically, these pebbled floors were made of black and white pebbles. The pebbles were mainly white but the detail of the flooring pattern was done with black pebbles and just inside the entrance doorway the date at which the flooring had been installed would be etched in black pebbles. Some of the old Greek properties that I would witness had this *khokaklia* dating back to the 17th century. The Captain had given one side to Kiki and building works were in progress to modernise it. I got called upon to provide a little labouring help, but this was the rub. We would be working at night as the work was being done without planning permission, and it was in full view of the Police Station at the top of the hill.

So this is the job. I have some help downstairs and we are producing mixer loads of cement and ballast and pouring it into containers.

When I spoke earlier of the antiquated building practices, this is on another level. The container that we were pouring the concrete into was a feta cheese tin which would probably have held about 10 litres. It was a square tin and on the inside of the tin, there was a short piece of wood that was nailed through the tin to a longer piece of wood. This would effectively create a double handle with which to pick up the tin of concrete. I would then hoist the tin onto my shoulder and carry it upstairs, in the dark, where Dimitris would be waiting on top of a ladder to pour the concrete into the wooden shuttering.

This went on for about three hours, during which time, we had several alarm calls to stop work as we thought we were being watched but then carried on.

With hindsight, I would say it was quite hard work, but I was young and fit and it didn't last long. At least it was at night when it was considerably cooler. The icing on the cake I suppose would have been when I was handed 15000 drachmas for my very short shift, or three days normal wages if you like. I finished my shift and went for a drink, the shoulders of my tee-shirt covered in concrete, as was my hair.

I was completely overwhelmed but I learnt something new that day. If you treat your staff with respect and pay them in accordance with the work they do, they will always come back and work for you again. I use that ethos in my business now in that my clients who pay promptly and without quibble will always get priority treatment in the future.

I need to set the record straight here. There is some sort of urban myth going around and it has been popularised by tourists repeating it to other tourists for the last thirty years or more. When you see a Greek building construction of one or two floors, but on the top floor, you can still see the steel reinforcement rods sticking out haphazardly from the roof in all four corners? The urban myth states that they leave it like that so they can class the building as unfinished and hence won't have to pay building taxes. Absolute tosh. It's left like that so that should they choose to extend upwards at any time, they can safely tie the new build in with the old.

Most Greeks didn't pay a drachma in tax until the mid-nineties anyway.

And there is no such thing as window tax. So just stop it with all your urban myths, please?

The summer approaches and I don't have a job.

It's April 1993. My mum and sister came out to visit me and I think mum was quite horrified at the person I had become. I recall little of their visit as I was drinking excessively. It had only been a few months since her last visit but I knew that she could see my decline. I had been celibate for around six months now. Not by choice of course but just as there hadn't been any opportunities and after what had been a fairly *active* summer I was finding it difficult to cope, and most likely resorting to drinking as a substitute.

Any seasonal tourist resort is hard to cope with if you are a twenty-something young man with an ever-increasing libido. The lack of female presence in the winter months can be hard to deal with. Tourists will eventually start to come back again but it's usually from April onwards. You will get the occasional lone traveller in March on an island hop but she will usually be a man-hating feminist or a lesbian and not worth the pursuance. Nothing wrong with being either of these obviously but I learned quickly to stop barking up the wrong tree.

Myself, Carl and Lee, we had managed to find ourselves some workers accommodation. I would describe it as an inner-city tower block but built on only two floors. It wasn't suitable for lease to the travel companies and as such, it was only let out to workers.

Three girls had turned up intending to open up a restaurant serving Mexican style food such as tortilla wraps and chilli-based food. It was novel and exciting as Lindos had no other facility to serve anything like this. It was all hot dogs, cheeseburgers, pitta gyros and chips until then and these girls raised a real interest locally. They decided to call this restaurant Alphabet Street and I helped out a little with the refurbishment of the property. It was in a prime location in that it was en route from the beach to the village and was a perfect halfway house for a drink and a little something different to eat. It also proved to be popular as an evening restaurant and they seemed to have cornered a different market. I never expected or wanted any financial recompense for any of the work that I had done for them as they would feed me for free on the many occasion I visited after their initial opening night.

This was the winter of discontent as far as the local police were concerned though. They had already had to deal with a mildly irritating English thug and his ex-marine mate and they suspected that the girls might be drug dealers or smugglers. The Police had been given information that three English girls were opening up a restaurant in town and they were keeping their drugs in an empty banana yoghurt pot. The Police turned up to investigate these allegations, and their best line of enquiry, after doing a sparse visual inspection was "where is your banana yoghurt?". Jo, one of the three replied coolly "we don't sell banana yoghurt", so the Police closed their investigations and left.

This was how The Police seemed to operate. They seemed to be fairly clueless and their default action, if they didn't get the answers they wanted, was just to beat people up although this would only ever happen to male *troublemakers.* They didn't seem to have the capacity to cope with anything other than sitting in a Police Station all day playing Backgammon or standing in the main square of Lindos directing traffic. National Service still exists in Greece, something that the UK could probably benefit from, and I learned that one of the ways to avoid being conscripted was to join The Police instead and I'm sure that many would have opted for this as an easier way of life. Of course, not all Greek policemen are this way inclined, but it just seemed that those who worked in small island resorts were.

The Alphabet Street girls had a chef in the restaurant called Rudy, a Mancunian lad. The only thing I properly remember about him was he used to have a bottle of beer in his back pocket which was connected by a series of straws so that he could drip-feed himself with alcohol while he worked. Legend.

Carl managed to get himself involved with one of the three girls and I was happy for him. I could see my life going off the rails, however. I was drinking excessively as I needed a comfort blanket. Supermarket beers were considerably lower priced than the local bars and it was very easy to get wasted for about £5 in equivalent money. My life was swimming around me with no proper sense of direction or future and I didn't want to admit defeat by simply packing up and going home to a life uncertain. Besides anything else, my pot was low and I couldn't even afford a flight.

Mum and sister left and the next night I was having a drink in the 60s Bar. Chris and Chris, the two business partners that had previously leased the business had left town owing a lot of money to both the 60s Bar and Pallas Taverna and the owner of the 60s Bar had resumed control. I knew him and he knew me. I had done a little work for him over the winter so I classed him as a friend. I took my drink and paid my drachmas and went to sit down in the outside area. It was or just seemed like a normal preseason night out in Lindos. With hindsight, I now realise that he didn't look comfortable and something was wrong.

He was sweating profusely and I was getting mixed signals and little eye contact from him. I'd only been there a few minutes when a uniformed copper marched in and cuffed me. Come with me was all he said and without protest, I followed him to the station.

When I got there I was placed down in front of the Chief of Police. Given the trouble that these five English boys had already caused him so far, I deduced that he wasn't about to invite me back to his house for dinner with his family and I was in some sort of trouble although I didn't know what I was alleged to have done. If being frequently pissed in a Greek holiday resort is a crime then they would have had a very long charge sheet.

The Chief of Police spoke English. It was adequate but he wasn't completely confident and would need a translator if he was replied to. It was at this moment that the owner of the 60s Bar entered. The Chief of Police said something to him and, the owner of the bar, who spoke excellent English, translated to me.

"Why did you break into my bar?", he asked.

I've done some things in my time when drunk but breaking and entering isn't one of them.

When Chris and Chris left at the end of the previous season I had the keys to the bar for a short while. I cleared it up and cleaned it down and then surrendered the keys to another local who was supposed to run the bar for the winter. That never happened as there wouldn't be enough bodies in the village to justify opening. One of my summer jobs, when I had been working at Pallas Taverna, was to go up to the bar in the afternoon before it opened and clean it. The bar had more or less been cleaned the previous night but this would just entail restocking the fridges and hosing down the bar floor. Many Greek buildings have natural drainage in that any floors or courtyards you hose down will just run into the streets and dry almost instantly in the afternoon sun.

"Why would I break into your bar?", I asked, perplexed. "I thought I was your friend?".

He said something to the Chief and I was signalled to leave.

They would come for me again but not for a few years.

I was starting to think I had made a mistake

in hanging around for the Winter as, apart from the occasional good day, it had been pretty disastrous up until now. What was so bad about life in England after all? A centrally heated house, a meal cooked every evening by mum, a circle of good friends and the opportunity to earn more than £15 a day. I couldn't back out now though as I'd survived this winter so far and it could only get better, or so I hoped.

As my hopes reached an all-time low, I heard on the grapevine that there was a job available in a hotel just on the outskirts of Lindos. It was for a live-in barman/handyman/maintain the rooms sort of position. I had all these skills as I was a qualified electrician with abilities in other areas and I'd done bar work in my earlier years. I actually just needed to get out of the village and off of the police radar.

I was hired immediately by a Greek man who spoke the absolute Queens English and

I felt like I had a purpose. I moved into the staff accommodation which was nothing more than two small rooms with an outside kitchenette and a shower room which I would have to share with Tracey, who had already been working there for a year or more.

1993 was just about to get underway.

Chapter Four

Season Two: Lindos Gardens

This seemed like the ideal job for me. I had finally found my niche. It was preseason and there was a lot of work to be done in the hotel before its opening day and the first tourists would arrive. The apartments needed painting, the electrics needed fixing, there was a lot of cleaning up to do and the swimming pool that had been empty in the winter needed a bloody good clean and it required a new coat of rubberised paint.

I think this was the only swimming pool in Greece that employed this version of waterproofing instead of the modern method of tiling.

For the first time in my stay in Lindos, I

had secured rent-free accommodation but I won't lie, it was basic. It was a purpose-built staff accommodation, and it wasn't at all salubrious. I had a small room with a single bed. The room next to mine was Tracey's. She had been working there the year before. There was a shared toilet/shower room that was outside of the two rooms but it was hardly ensuite. We had to walk out of our respective rooms into the open air and then the *bathroom* would be there. It had no hot water connected to it and there was a kitchenette unit outside the bathroom which contained a fridge and two electric cooking rings. Neither of these was of any use as they weren't connected to any electrical supply. Our best hope for a hot shower would be later on in the season when the underground water supply feeding the bathroom had warmed up sufficiently to allow about a minutes worth of hot water before running cold again. Before this time, we would befriend the guests and blag a shower in their rooms as, even though it was all solar-heated water, in the early months it was all barely above tepid and we would have to switch on the electrical backup.

It was early April and the charter flights hadn't started coming in yet but we were ready to open and we had a few guests staying that had just happened to find us. They were island hopping I think. It gets dark and cold very early at that time of year but the small bar that we had at the hotel had sliding glass doors and we had some really fun nights in there, often going on until the early hours of the morning.

My duties were simple. I would do the room maintenance in the daytime and I would be running the bar at night. I was responsible for making sure the pool was clean and chlorinated and that the guests were happy. Tracey would do the bar shift during the day and the laundry, ie the bed linen, pillowcases etc.

Louise, who was an English girl but going out with a local Greek, cleaned the rooms on a rota basis, dependant on arrival days and how long the rooms had been occupied. Louise would also do an evening bar shift occasionally to give me a night off although I would just spend the night in the bar anyway. I was getting to like this job. It had everything I needed and I was starting to save some money again. We were paid weekly instead of daily but it was always on time and always on the same day. The wages, at 4000 drachmas per day and for seven days a week were 1000 drachmas lower than the going rate anywhere else but at least the accommodation was free and that in itself was a saving.

I'd come from a self-employed background and was used to being my own boss. Tracey and I were left to run the place as we pleased and we were trusted. My only gripe, and it was something that I hadn't previously experienced, was that we had to write down any drinks from the bar we had in a book which was known as the Bar Maison, and this would be deducted from our wages. It didn't really matter as we were bought so many drinks by customers that we were actually in credit most nights. If a customer offered to buy us a drink we would graciously accept and then ring the customers' drinks through the till but put their contribution into the tips jar which we would divvy up regularly.

I had a side business in that, and this was totally with the owner's approval as he had suggested it, that I could sell cigarettes from behind the bar. I would go down to the village and buy cartons of 200 of the most popular brands and sell them to customers at 50 drachmas above the packet price. In Greece, the pricing is controlled by the Greek Government. The price is clearly printed on the packet and you'll never pay any more than that, unlike our system where convenience stores and motorway service stations can invent their prices as they know, for the most part, that a smoker will go to the ends of the earth and spend their last pennies on cigarettes if they have run out of their favourite fix.

If you've ever walked down from the top of Lindos into the village – and back again - you'll understand why 50 drachmas is a bargain. In all honesty, it was worth little more than about 20p in English money in those times. Cigarettes in Greece in the 90s were the equivalent of one English pound a packet. My cigarette business was thriving.

I would also do my best to promote businesses outside of Lindos Gardens that weren't a threat to our own business. I need to rephrase that in that if someone wanted to know which the best restaurant was to go to in town or where there were activities such as water sports I would do my best to give them the best information. I knew John, an English guy who had a Parascending business on the Pallas Beach. I would regularly advise our customers of this, without ever knowing if they had taken my advice. At the end of the season, John invited me down for a free parascend as I'd sent a lot of business his way that year. I had no idea. No one had ever come back to me to tell me how much they had enjoyed it. Or perhaps they hadn't?

I also had a car or the use of one at the very least. It was more of a Mini Moke than a car and it didn't have windows apart from the windscreen. It just had a throw over cover with clear panels in it. Lindos Gardens was situated at the top of the hill outside Lindos. The walk up from the village was hard going even for fit and active people and as there were no restaurant facilities at the complex, we were finding that guests were going down to the village and staying there in the evening and getting a taxi back much later. As a result, the bar was often quiet in the evenings and takings were low.

I had this ingenious idea that we should run a taxi service from 9 to 9:30 every evening where we would pick up guests and bring them back free as long as they had prebooked. My plan worked and the bar started to get busy in the evenings again.

I recall two families were staying with us, and the male counterparts were good friends and they liked a drink or two. Our bar prices were expensive though. Much more than the village prices, even though drink prices in the 90s weren't as eye-watering as they are now.

Malcolm and Duncan – or Malc The Alc and Dunc The Drunk as I renamed them – hatched a plan with me. They suggested I buy a bottle of 5* Metaxa from a supermarket in the village and keep it behind the bar. I was to charge them every time they wanted a drink but at a significantly reduced rate and I could keep all the profit. Their wives and kids were still buying drinks from the bar but not in the same volumes as these two. This worked a treat as the boss was never around in the evenings so he was none the wiser.

Every arrival day, which would be a Saturday or a Wednesday, there would be a welcome meeting with the Thomson travel rep. I would line up trays of complimentary drinks for the new arrivals and after the well-versed speech from the rep I would hand out the drinks. I saw a new opportunity opening. As my duties were to maintain the rooms and make sure they were fit for arrival I saw a master plan. I would be given a list of rooms that needed to be prepared and checked.

I would survey the list of incoming guests

and make a mental note of the rooms that contained all female parties. I would then leave something in the room that needed fixing or attending to. Something simple such as a blown light bulb or a blocked sink or toilet. I proceeded to advise the Thomson rep that she needed to elaborate her speech somewhat to include the instruction that *if you have any issues with your room please contact our head of maintenance, Chris, and he will do his best to resolve those issues as soon as possible.* She would then gesture towards the bar where I would be stood and I would give a silent wave to the guests as acknowledgement.

It was a crass move on my part but it worked in my favour. In my stupid twenty-seven year old, testosterone-fuelled imagination, I thought that if I responded to their requests as soon as possible then they might just come into the bar that night and buy me a drink as a thank you for sorting out the blocked drain or getting their hairdryer working or getting rid of the fucking mahoosive spider that was crawling around their apartment, and I might get sexual favours as a result.

While I realise that this sort of behaviour makes me seem like I was some sort of predatory sex offender, this really wasn't the case, but, the thing about this notion of mine was that it was actually proving to be productive. I would watch these parties of girls throughout the evening, not as a stalker, obviously, but just casually observing, until such a time as they'd all retired to their rooms and the last remaining member would sit at the bar opposite me and the inevitable would happen. It had started out with me targeting them but in the end, they had singled me out and the whole process had been reversed.

I said I wouldn't go into specific details about individual conquests and that won't change but I felt a shift of power. Suddenly, it was me that was doing the groundwork and getting a reward for my efforts. The boss completely approved of my *work* as only a Greek man could and I was regularly applauded by him for my achievements.

Life in Lindos can change in a day. Somewhere, just around the corner, there is someone you had never met when you were not even looking for them when you woke up that morning, but they will come along and they will change your life, and this finally happened to me.

Using the same tactics as I had employed before, I noticed there was an incoming female party that was sharing one of our four-bed apartments. I made a mental note, in my head, but I wasn't really prepared for what turned up. They were four beautiful girls, in their twenties and just about the same age group as me, or so I perceived. I was completely spoilt for choice but there was one who caught my eye.

She was the most beautiful girl I had ever set my eyes upon at that point in my life. She had delicious locks of dark hair, wonderful olive skin and sultry dark eyes. So when I witnessed her ushering her mates back to the room and making her way to the bar, which I was just about to close for the night, I honestly couldn't believe my luck. We chatted for a couple of hours before we realised it was getting into the early hours of the morning and we decided to retire to my shabby apartment. It didn't put her off though as she spent the rest of her holiday with me, and I realised that I'd just stupidly fallen in love again.

I've never really understood why any woman or girl would be attracted to a man who was over six feet tall and built like a stick insect, and I promise you, nothing has changed to this day, but I suppose back then, I had an amazing golden tan, sun-bleached blonde hair and a ponytail which reached almost halfway down the length of my back and I must have been the epitome of what an English worker in the 90s was supposed to look like.

Sunday was my day off, in the daytime anyway, as Sunday evenings were for the weekly barbeque. These were fun evenings and usually well attended. The party games would ensue after the food was done with and these progressed to more adult games when the families had retired for the evening.

I suggested to Rachel, for that was her name, that we take the Mini Moke and go out for the day somewhere. It was the last Sunday of her two-week stay and she was leaving on the impending Wednesday. I drove us to Agathi Beach a few kilometres north of Lindos and we spent the day in the glorious sunshine laying on the sunbeds and swimming in the crystal clear water. I had never been in a situation like this before with anyone and it just felt that she was the one for me, despite the fact we had only known each other for a little over a week

Rachel left on the transfer bus at the end of her holiday and I could not believe this was happening. I genuinely thought that like me, she had come to Lindos to find love, a better life, and a more secure future. I really just wanted her to throw away her return ticket and stay forever as I had done. But we exchanged postal addresses and as she left on the transfer bus, I'm not ashamed to say that I cried a lot, especially as I could witness her through the window of the bus with tears in her eyes. Before my tears had properly dried I went back to my shitty room and started to compose a letter.

Despite the frustratingly slow Greek postal system, we managed to write to each other twice a week and we sent each other parcels with mixtape compilations so we could compare our musical tastes. I was quickly falling in love with Rachel and even though my heart was already sold to Lindos and I was thinking about a permanent life there, someone had just turned up, swept me off my feet and then left as quickly as she had arrived and, by doing so, had left a massive hole in my life that couldn't be filled, unless I returned to the UK permanently. The problem was, there was still two months of the season to fulfil and I wanted to do this. The fact that we kept in contact assured me everything would be ok.

My season at Lindos Gardens hadn't ended well. There was a pretty monumental storm at the end of the season after all the guests had left, although not as vociferous as we would learn that would arrive just a year later. Vassilis, the owner, turned up just as I was about to leave for my flight home and started instructing me to cover the areas that were susceptible to leaks. I give him a sign of dismissal before I jumped into the taxi bound for Rhodes Airport and a better life.

I had achieved all I had come here to do. I was over my first girlfriend, she didn't matter anymore. I had more than coveted myself in terms of conquests and I was ready to move on. Rachel was the girl I wanted to spend the rest of my life with and she could have my babies if she wanted.

Rachel met me at 4 am at Gatwick Airport. It was the only flight I could get or afford. She drove us to her house, or it was her mother's house anyway. I met her mother later in the morning when we had finally woken up and her mother took to me instantly. I think she wanted her daughter to produce grandchildren straight away. I spent a few wonderful days with her and then caught the train home to announce to my mum that I had met someone and was coming home for good. Mum was pleased for me. I resumed my life as an electrician and I was finding steady work. I bought a cheap car to run around and go to work and to drive over to see Rachel. Life was good but one of my old habits was starting to rear its ugly head again.

I would see Rachel fairly regularly over the next month or so but in the times we were apart it would have made sense to phone her. Mobile phones weren't a thing back then and we take social media for granted these days for its ease of non-face to face communication. My parents had a house phone though, for God's sake. It was on the telephone table, just inside the front door, in the hallway, at the bottom of the stairs, where I would have to walk past every night before going to bed, after having been out drinking with my mates. Maybe I should have phoned her more often. I would just spend our time apart drinking with my mates and then going to see her at weekends. In hindsight, I guess I just suppose I thought that was how long-distance relationships worked.

The last time I saw Rachel was probably mid-December. I had gone down to see her but I sensed something was wrong as the closeness wasn't there. Before the day was out she announced that she didn't feel our relationship was working and she wanted to call it a day. To say that I was gutted was an understatement, but I managed to hold my tears back and I accepted her decision. Trying to hold on to someone who doesn't want to be with you is pointless and you end up bitter and hating them for it. I wanted to remember the Rachel I had fallen in love with.

Christmas is looming and I'm certainly not going to spend another Christmas in Lindos but with no real reason to be in the UK anymore, I started to make plans. Life at home had moved on anyway. One of my old drinking mates admitted to me that he was now seeing my ex-girlfriend. I told him I wasn't bothered and he was free to do what he liked but I was angry and resentful although there was no reason for me to feel that way as it had been nearly two years already.

I sent Rachel a video of The Jungle Book for Christmas – it was a film she was obsessed with - and she sent me a Zippo lighter, ironically, as I knew she didn't like the fact that I was a smoker.

Once again, my objectives had changed. I had bought all my possessions home with me thinking that my time in Lindos was done but I had to rethink my future. Should I stay in the UK and get a proper job? I had been working for an old electrician friend of mine and he was giving me a weeks work at a time, cash in hand, and I was saving again but the lure of spending eleven months of the year in the sun was calling again so by mid-January I am already making plans to go again. This time, I would be carrying a toolkit of sorts in my luggage and that would mean a decent claw hammer, a pair of electrical side-cutters and some decent screwdrivers, as well as my Hitachi hammer drill and an extension lead. I would eventually convert this extension lead and replace the 13a plug with a Continental plug so that it could be plugged into a Greek socket without the need for a travel adaptor.

Get your arse ready Lindos. I'm coming back and this time it's with a vengeance and a purpose.

Chapter Five

Season Three: A Year of Mixed Fortunes

It was late January when I eventually returned. I'd carried on working in the UK for a bit longer just to build up some more cash reserves as I wasn't sure if I'd be working at Lindos Gardens again. I felt fairly sure there was a job there for me but Tracey had left at the end of the 93 season and wasn't coming back so it would have a very different feel.

I was becoming a familiar face amongst the locals mainly because you become more prominent in a village with a small population when there are no tourists. It's easy to be inconspicuous in a busy summer when the resort is flooded with English workers and tourists of course.

I wasn't short of work in terms of preparing properties for the summer ahead and my skills as an electrician were becoming recognised and generally my ability to fix or repair things that were broken. I could get paid more for something like replacing a water heater tank than I would for an entire day in a restaurant or wherever.

Carl and Lee had gone back to the UK sometime in the previous season, never to return to work in Lindos again but Martin was still around and working for Patric Walker as his Man Friday, so to speak. I got to meet Patric several times as I did some electrical work for him in the house that he owned, and I found him to be a delightfully funny and intelligent man. I lunched with him and Martin on several occasions and the dinner conversation would be hilarious. He was not afraid to use the *C word*, whatever company he was in. Martin had certainly landed on his feet here. I sort of wish now that I could have asked Patric to predict my future for me but, as we all know, that Astrology is a load of bollocks.

Patric had spent the latter years of his life in seclusion in Lindos as he had become tired of people at parties asking him to guess their astrological sign.

It seems incredible now to think that within a year or so from that point in time, he would be dead from the effects of salmonella food poisoning at the mere age of 64.

I can't completely recall where I was staying for those early months. Martin did put me up in his house for a while and it was a house and not just a room. It was paid for by Patric, whose house was just around the corner. I can remember every accommodation I have ever lived in so I'll just have to assume that I stayed with Martin for some time.

By now, it was late March and I didn't really have a plan for the summer ahead. I was over Rachel, which in fairness, didn't take long as the split was amicable and we didn't have any further contact with each other. Unlike in the past, I didn't bother to stalk her in terms of calling her "out of the blue, just for a friendly chat, to see if we were still friends", as I had done in the past when I was unable to let a girl go, without a fight at least.

I resigned myself to the fact that I would possibly be working at Lindos Gardens again. It was familiar territory, I knew the job well, and I had free accommodation so it was a win-win situation.

I went up to see if I could find Vassilis. He lived in Haraki but I figured that as it was about this time last year that I had been up to enquire about the job that he would be there again.

I was astonished at what I found. He had lost a considerable amount of weight, completely shaved the ridiculous bushy beard that he used to sport and his hair had been cropped short. He looked ten years younger. I learned that his wife had divorced him over the winter and taken him for a lot of money. I expect his new look was so that he could go out and play the field again.

"I'm back", I announced. He smiled warmly and shook my hand. "Welcome", he said. "We've got plenty of work to do here".

I looked at my watch. It was already midday.

"I'll be here first thing in the morning. I assume I still have my room?"

"Of course", he smiled.

I complimented him on his new youthful looks and he smiled again. He seemed a lot happier in himself so I could only hope for a good season ahead.

I asked if I could take the Moke to go and collect my stuff and he obliged. I didn't really need to move in as it was rent-free at Martin's but it made more sense to wake up on the hotel site in the morning to be ready for work. The Moke hadn't moved since the time I'd last parked it, but it fired into life with the first turn of the key and it felt good to have my *wheels* back. I always doubted if that car was roadworthy or even legal.

I recall an instance the previous season when I had been doing my taxi runs. I used to pick up a family of four every night who, to be frank, looked as though the walk up the hill would have been more beneficial to them. They were mum, dad and two daughters in their mid-teens and they were very large. Morbidly obese would be the medical term I guess. I secretly renamed them The

GoLightly's which I'm fairly sure was a reference to someone in Noel's House Party, but I can't be positive so don't quote me on that.

Every time I drove them back up the hill, their total combined weight would cause the prop shaft of the rear-wheel drive Moke to pop out about halfway up the hill. I had to manually locate it back into position and then take them two at a time.

I eventually decided to effect some sort of rudimentary repair by lashing it in with some steel wire that I'd found in my *tool shed* at the hotel but it would persistently break after a few days or more until the point that I had to ask Vassilis to get it repaired properly in a garage. I think, apart from putting fuel into it, that was the only other money he spent on that jalopy. I loved it though. It gave me freedom and mobility and I would occasionally pay for the fuel myself.

The month ahead before the season started was full-on with lots to do and a few Albanians were helping out as well. I didn't spend any time in the hotel in the evening as there was nothing there for me. The bar hadn't been stocked and I was alone there in the evenings so I would just go down to the village for a drink. There were a few bars open and a few English workers already in town so it made sense to socialise that way. They weren't boozy nights out as in my laziness I would take the Moke rather than walk home. I would undoubtedly have been over the limit but drink driving in Greece seemed to be a national pastime so I would never worry about being stopped.

We got the place ready and it looked fantastic. I'd installed floodlights on the walls of the two-storey apartments to illuminate the pool at night and the swimming pool that we had scrubbed clean and repainted again looked magnificent with its crystal clear water. I don't know if that pool ever got tiled but it would have made more sense in the long term. Next door to the hotel was a small farm holding and the owner would regularly forget to shut his gates and his cows would *escape.* It wasn't an uncommon sight to see cows aimlessly wandering around the hotel area and occasionally around the pool. I dread to think what would have happened if one of them had accidentally stumbled into the pool. Apart from the obvious fact that it would have drowned, I've no idea how we would have ever got it out.

The early season was easy as we weren't fully booked and we could pretty much manage the place between us but I warned Vassilis that we would need to start hiring an extra pair of hands soon. Lindos Gardens has expanded phenomenally now but back then it was just a complex of twenty three apartments with a pool, an all-day bar, and no restaurant. We didn't do much in the way of bar snacks apart from cheese and ham toasties and we had these pre-prepared meals which arrived frozen and we would cook them through in the small portable electric oven that we had behind the bar. It was the standard moussaka/pastitsio sort of thing and it seemed popular. There was a small shop on site where the guests could buy basics and some re-frigerated food for self-catering. We did have fresh veg and fruit so it wasn't all bad.

The company that supplied us the frozen meals went by the name of όμορφος or, Omorfos, as it is pronounced. The Greek guy who ran the company called himself Sam, but I guessed he was probably a Tsam-bicos. He was an amicable sort of fellow and we got on really well, mainly as he spoke good English and my Greek was still a bit limited. I was getting better with it but not confident enough to hold a full conversation.

One day, he gave me a tee-shirt with the company name emblazoned across the front. I still had no idea what it meant but I thought it looked cool to have a tee shirt with Greek writing on it. If I didn't know what it meant then it would be unlikely that an English tourist would know.

I went down into the village one evening wearing this tee shirt and as I walked through the streets, the slightly less mature young waiters who were standing on the terraces of the restaurants and tavernas started cheering me and laughing and blowing me kisses then calling out to their friends further down to alert them of what, or who was coming. I had no idea what was going on, other than the fact that the hilarity was aimed at me.

I thought nothing more of it and put it to the back of my mind. A few days later Sam came with a new delivery for us and I casually asked him what Omorfos meant.

"Ah, it means beautiful", he replied with a smile, and then the penny dropped. I knew that Greek words could be gender-specific such as in other languages but not English.

Omorfos could also be pronounced Omorfi without changing the meaning but it would make it female. So I was walking through the streets telling everyone that I was a beautiful boy. I didn't wear that tee shirt in public again.

I apologise, I've gone off on a tangent somewhat.

Vassilis suggested I go on the lookout for an extra member of staff so I put the word around the village. I had a dilemma though because Tracey would be irreplaceable. I loved her to bits as she was a good worker and we made a great team and I felt that only a bloke would be able to handle the workload that she had previously coped with. My issue with that was that I would have competition with him and no exclusivity on the female guests. I had decided to forget about trying to meet anyone as I was going to revert to my former behaviour.

A fella who was about my age, but most likely younger, turned up, enquiring about the job. I honestly don't remember his name but he was a Northerner and he looked a bit shifty. He probably would have been more suited to Faliraki. It wasn't my responsibility to employ him so I introduced him to Vassilis who had a brief chat with him and he was hired. I sort of wished I'd had some sort of say in the decision as I didn't really like him from the start. There was something about him that suggested he might not be good for the business.

But to hand it to him, he was a good looking lad. He was already tanned and a bit swarthy and I reckoned he'd draw the girls in. I'd be quite happy to take any cast-offs as although I did have certain standards, I wasn't overly fussy. I wasn't looking for long term partners anymore.

He would do the day shift on the bar which would free me up for my basic maintenance duties and leave me with a generally easy day with various rest moments to conserve my energy for the evening shift which would finish when the last person left.

I don't ever recall him using Tracey's old room even though it was there for him. I certainly would have remembered him being there if he had so I can only assume he had accommodation elsewhere, or that Vassilis hadn't given him that option. He had a friend who he had travelled with though and I do remember that he was called Simon. I would often see Simon sitting at the end of the bar with a drink or actually standing behind the bar which was not a situation that Vassilis would have approved of. I had to ask him on more than one occasion to remove himself and I'm sure that he was probably being given free drinks.

The beauty of this job was that I'd come from a self-employed background and I was used to being my own boss. The fact that Vassilis wasn't around much during the day, and less so in the evenings meant that I had the freedom to run the place as I wanted to and I was starting to develop an affection for it.

It was quite early on in the season and a family of three turned up. I was fairly surprised as the daughter looked to be about my age and holidaying with my parents if I had already reached that age wouldn't even be a consideration. They didn't look very happy either but that wasn't an uncommon sight. Some people don't do the travel element of a foreign holiday very well or their accommodation isn't what they were expecting or, actually, for any number of reasons. As their holiday progressed, they started to engage a little more.

My couple of seasons in Lindos had given me more confidence to socialise with people generally, and I liked to get to know people and a little of their background, musical tastes, football team, etcetera. I had become a good listener and a good conversationalist. I was doing my rounds and I saw her sat in the bar area on her own with a drink. I had half an hour to spare so I politely asked if I could join her, to which she graciously accepted. I had no ulterior motive here. I was just being friendly. We chatted for a while and then I went about my business.

She came into the bar later when I was doing my evening shift and we chatted again. It was during this conversation that the reason for their apparent *unhappiness* became clear. She revealed to me that all three of them had been the victims of a horrific family tragedy. To this day, what happened is still beyond comprehension to me so I can't even begin to imagine what they were going through.

There's no need for me to go into any more detail than that as anyone who knows Sarah will know all the facts.

We chatted a lot over the remainder of her stay there and this is where my memory gets a little cloudy. I don't remember if it was me who suggested that she come and work for a season or if it was her suggestion and if there were any jobs available at Lindos Gardens. The result of this was that I had a word with Vassilis and he was happy to take her on but the other lad would have to go. That didn't bother me as I had no rapport with him and I didn't really like him.

Sarah had to return to the UK first to prepare herself for a summer season abroad. When John...it's starting to come back to me now...yes, his name was John. When John got wind of this he knew, or he guessed he was being replaced, and he left shortly afterwards.

Vassilis went to pick her up from the airport. It was late and I don't remember if the bar was still open when she got back or if I had closed up and gone to bed, mainly because at this point in time, such an event was insignificant.

One of Sarah's first questions to me, as I welcomed her back, was *it normal for Greek men to try it on with their female staff?* I wasn't surprised by this but horrified that he would even consider such a move knowing Sarah's recent events. I had explained the situation to him beforehand.

Vassilis was starting to go off the rails a little. His newfound youth and vitality, and possibly his reawakened libido meant that he was getting his share of the female guests. Fortunately, the age group of his targets were not of the age group I had previously been interested in. There were a couple of friends who were in their fifties who were holidaying at the hotel. They were attractive and classy in a MILF sort of way, and Vassilis had managed to latch himself onto one of them. She spent most of her holiday in his apartment in Haraki while her friend slept alone at the hotel.

They both lived in Chiswick, Greater London. Shortly after their stay at Lindos Gardens, he travelled back to the UK to see her. I had to laugh though as Vassilis was fluent in English. There honestly wasn't a word you could trip him up on but he couldn't pronounce Chiswick. He called it Chis Wick.

She travelled back with him and bought her daughter Suzy with her who came to work with me and Sarah. Suzy was lovely, if a little ditzy. I didn't really get to know her that well as my time at Lindos Gardens would be short-lived.

I learned later that when his *girlfriend* had returned with him, he would lock her in his apartment in Haraki while he was out. She eventually managed to free herself and fled back to Chis Wick.

Before this happened, Sarah and I had become an item. I don't know how or why or what led up to it but I guess, despite my intention to remain single and available I suppose I needed someone and I suppose she did too.

Sarah moved into my room and we appropriated a double bed from an apartment that had two double beds. It was only classed as a 3 bedroomed apartment anyway and was only ever used by a family of mum, dad, and one offspring.

Vassilis was also obsessed with the fact that his staff were stealing from him. He muttered several times about installing cameras behind the bar, which I found offensive. The worst thing I'd ever done was sell a few bottles of Metaxa 5* at a bit of profit and that was only a week's worth of private business. Anything other than that had always been completely above board.

He would go through the till receipts as everything was itemised as beer, spirits, soft drinks, etcetera.

He knew that a barrel of draught Amstel contained x amount of litres so he couldn't understand why the figures didn't add up and why he wasn't getting the exact return on his beer barrels. He had obviously never heard of wastage, spillage, or the fact that when the gas is too high, it takes a bit more to get a full glass.

This wasn't even his most bizarre behaviour. I would prefer to describe this as atrocious and irresponsible. He came in one morning with a puppy. I don't know what breed it was but it was hardly likely it would have been a pedigree. It was completely black with short wiry hair.

He handed me the puppy and said, "This is your dog. Feed it, give it a name, and look after it".

At that point in my life, I had never had a dog as a pet, and neither had my parents. We were *cat people.* I was fucking furious. I had absolutely no idea what to do with it but I gave it a name at least. I decided to call it Mavrikos as *mavros* is the Greek word for black and when you give it a gender, male as it was, it becomes Mavrikos. I fed it scraps from the barbecue, used hotel funds to buy tins of crappy dog food from the supermarkets but as I had no experience with dogs or puppies, I knew nothing of behaviour training or how important it is to give a dog the correct diet in the correct weight proportions in their formative years. This was something I would be more aware of when I would meet my future wife......spoiler alert.

Vassilis also employed a Greek man from Malona to assist me in the bar in the evenings. Dimitri or *Jimmy* as he preferred to call himself was his name. This would prove to be a mistake. He would drink most of the profits and jump on his motorbike at the end of his shift and race home to his home village of Malona to his English girlfriend. The fact that he had survived a near-fatal crash some years earlier where he had careered off the road whilst drunk and hit a rock hadn't taught him anything about the perils of excessive drink driving. It all came to a head one night in the bar when we got into a disagreement over something or other and he pulled a knife on me in full view of the customers. He was sacked the next day. I bumped into him a few years later when I was holidaying in Pefkos, a resort a little further south of Lindos. He had his own bar by then. No prizes for guessing the name of the bar. Answers on a postcard, please. We shook hands and hugged. I doubt if he even remembers what happened that night.

I received a letter from my sister saying that she was coming over to see me. I was made up. I'd already had a visit from mum and dad and my brother and another visit when she came out with mum a few months later, and I'd seen her when I'd been back in the UK in the winter months but this was her first time in Lindos on her own. She was my rock. She had supported me emotionally when I was at my lowest after my split with my first girlfriend in the UK. I missed her terribly so this would be a chance to catch up. At this point, I had no intention of leaving Lindos. I managed to get her a free room at Martin's accommodation and did my best to make sure she was well looked after during her stay. I used as much spare time as I could to take her around the village and meet my friends and take her to restaurants where we could eat well. Vassilis said she could attend and eat at the Barbeque for free. He had a good heart and good intentions.

When you are promised a visit from a family member, the first thing you think of is what can they bring you from the UK that is difficult to buy in Greece. I needed a CD/tape player with speakers, the detachable type, not an all-in-one ghetto blaster. I met my sister at Rhodes Airport, and I'm ashamed to say the first thing I was interested in was whether she had managed to get me CD/cassette player. She had managed to but I'd forgotten how difficult it is to transport an extra item with all your usual luggage. At least now I had a medium on which to play my mixtapes and CD's that I had brought over. I will be forever thankful for that. Love you, sis.....xxx

I arranged with the Thomson reps that she could travel on the transfer coach back to Rhodes Airport. This saved us both from a journey of emotional torture in a taxi. It is now illegal to travel on transfer coaches unless you are holidaying with the travel company. Essentially it's for insurance purposes. I was glad to have the opportunity to watch her leave as I could go back to my room. When she left after her holiday I cried for hours.

Things were getting busy at the hotel. It was 1994 and the World Cup was in progress. This was when Vassilis had decided to fly back to Chis Wick, England, to see his girlfriend. Sunday Barbeque was cancelled as he wouldn't be there and I had no idea where he bought the meat from but I had a better plan.

I drove over to Lardos where I knew there was a good butcher and I bought as many pork souvlakis as I could. I also went to the supermarket and bought as much fresh salad produce as I could. I advertised it in the bar as Souvlaki Salad and Soccer night. I hate the term Soccer but it was the three S's. I pitched the cost at 2000 drachmas per person which was 3000 drachmas below the regular price for Barbeque Sunday and it was at zero profit on food, it was just to cover the costs.

Ireland was playing and we had a crappy old cathode ray tube TV in the bar area on which you couldn't see the screen in the daytime but as the evening drew in the picture became more visible. The reception wasn't great and it was hardly Ultra 4kHD but it was adequate and we didn't have any form of Sky Sports subscription so it had Greek commentary.

Oh my fucking days.

We just had the best night ever in that bar. We ran out of beer twice, and both times I had to jump in the Moke and drive down to Keith at The Parking Place to grab a barrel of beer from him, despite being fairly pissed myself. I pulled the Zeta reading off the till at the end of the night and placed it in an envelope with all the receipts for the food and the two chitty notes from Keith. We had doubled the best ever bar takings in all my time there.

I first started work when I was thirteen years old doing a paper round. I worked on market stalls before leaving school and in between leaving school and starting an apprenticeship I had a summer job. I've been self-employed for longer than I care to remember and I've always had the ability to generate money. I can run a business, as I still do to this day, and I can look after a business. I grew up in the 1970s when you made your own way in life, unlike the privileged children of today. I'm proud of my heritage and my upbringing.

Vassilis returned a few days later and called me into the office. He enquired about how it had been during his absence. I Informed him it had been busy and pointed him towards Sunday's takings. I expected him to be pleased and I expected to be congratulated but he said nothing, not even a thank you. I was confused by his reaction. He was obsessed with money and profit. Was it that I was apparently running his business better than he could?

If you've ever been in a situation where you've done something extracurricular for your employer but have had no reward or gratitude for your efforts you can appreciate that this was a monumental kick in the balls for me.

However, not to be undone by this lack of

appreciation, I took it on the chin and left his office with a different perspective.

A couple of days later, the events of the last few days and the sheer process of organising an event that had been so successful had started to take its toll on me and I was physically and emotionally drained. I went for an afternoon siesta before the evening duties were to resume and, after a couple of hours, maybe, I was awoken by Sarah.

She began her rhetoric.

"I've just been called into the office by Vassilis", she started.

"He says you're not working hard enough and you're not up to speed. He says that if you don't improve within 48 hours you will be replaced."

To this day, I don't know if Vassilis was playing mind games with me but it was all the ammunition I needed. I had a quick discussion with Sarah about our future and we agreed on a plan of action. I took a trip down to the beach to see Cliff and Rena. The nature of my job meant that I was a rare visitor to the beach these days and something of a stranger to those shores.

"Pubman, long time no see", Rena announced as I walked into the kitchen. "What can I get you?"

I probably need to explain the Pubman moniker here. It goes back to the first winter when we had all started socialising together in the evenings, something you don't get the opportunity to do in a busy summer. I think Martin was astounded at my capacity for alcohol as he wasn't a big drinker himself. He said something along the lines of:

 Look at you, Chris. I can just imagine you sat in a pub in England with your pint of beer and cigarettes and your darts laid out on the bar and your copy of The Racing Post open, studying the form. You are the original Pub Man.

That's not a verbatim quote but it is generally the gist of it and so the nickname stuck. Besides anything else, my nickname in the UK was *Stretch* at that time and still is now and there was already someone working in Lindos who went by the name of Stretch. He was an ex para I believe but therein lies a whole lot of other stories.

"Bacon butty and an Amstel, please. And a bit of help. I need a job and wonder if you knew of anything going."

"We've got a job here mate but it's a bit shit. We just need a washer upper", she replied. Tactful, honest, and on point as always.

That was all I needed to hear and I promised Rena I would be there in the morning. A long walk up the hill and an even longer search around the village for some suitably priced accommodation turned up some favourable results. I went back up to The Lindos Gardens to confront Vassilis.

"I understand you aren't happy with me and I have 48 hours to improve", was my opening gambit.

"Yes", he replied, without bothering to elaborate.

"I'd like to counter your offer and give you 48 minutes notice but I promise you I'll be gone in 45".

"You are replaceable", he countered further.

"Maybe so", I replied. "But when I leave, Sarah is coming with me".

The mind games continued. He told me to come back in a week and he would sort out the outstanding wages. I was expecting the worst and he didn't disappoint.

When I returned to collect what was owed he deducted the "free rent" I had been given over the last two years and it transpired that I owed him over 50,000 drachmas. Suffice to say I dismissed his allegations as bullshit and sour grapes, and I never saw him again, or at least not for a few more years. He also told the Chief of Police that he had sacked me as I had been stealing from him, as if I needed that can of worms reopening. I'd been fortunate enough to have worked there for a season and a half without any official work papers and I really didn't need the police on my back again.

When I left, Mavrikos was still a part of the hotel *family* and I use that term loosely. It would be unlikely that he would survive beyond a few years or even the coming winter as this was the way. I'm sorry for letting you down Mavrikos.

Sarah and I were sorted for accommodation and I had a job. Sarah got herself a job in a jewellery shop in the village. We seemed to be happy. Looking back now I don't know if Sarah was content in her employment. If she wasn't she never exhibited any signs towards me when we were together.

By comparison, I had landed a dream job. Being a washer upper is not a job I trained for at school but when you are working with a bunch of people who have a real zest for life it's easy to forget that you spend your entire day with your hands in hot soapy water cleaning up other people's mess and ketchup.

In front of Cliff and Rena's restaurant was a patch of sunbeds belonging to a local man, Dimitris Savaidis. I was hired to monitor these sunbeds and check for occupancy meaning that if someone took possession of the sunbed in the morning but then vacated it by the afternoon, I could charge again for the subsequent occupancy. This was too easy. I had two jobs running concurrently and I could easily manage them by using my downtime in between washing up cycles. I was on good money and I was being fed three times a day.

I had become something of a monetary whore.

How was I to know that this simple act of taking on a second job would impact my life in the season of 1995?

There are many stories that I could recount from my time working with Cliff and Rena and their daughter Natalie but you would do better to read Bob Penny's excellent book "The Life of Riley" if you haven't already done so,

The season is drawing to a close. It's late September and we - Sarah and myself - get the news that Sarah's mum is paying another visit, and this time she's bringing Sarah's sister. Her twin sister. Her *identical* twin sister. And her sisters' kids. I'm sure that parents can distinguish identical twins from one another but I genuinely couldn't. Sarah and I hired a car and we drove to Rhodes Airport to collect them. I drove back with Sarah's mum in the front seat and Sarah and Ruthie and the kids in the back. For the entire journey, I watched through the rearview mirror and listened to the two inseparable siblings catching up. It was like having Sarah in stereo.

The only difference was the skin tone. Sarah had tanned beautifully over the season but Ruthie was a pale English white. By the time Ruthie left, I couldn't tell the difference.

The memory goes cloudy again now. I think, and if you're reading this Sarah, you left with your mum and Ruthie and the kids on the return flight....correct me if I'm wrong.

I do know that when my parents turned up in late October for another visit you weren't around because you and my parents missed the most destructive storms that Lindos had witnessed for many a decade. I still have the old address book with its ink-stained pages where the rain was hammering down as I attempted to make some calls home from the telephone in the main square of Lindos.

The weather had turned unseasonable. The sky had turned darker than usual and there were spots of rain in the air. In a long hot and dry summer, we would always welcome a shower to refresh the air and let us breathe again. Bob Penny was living with his girlfriend/eventually to become his wife. They had vacated their room to return home and, as Sarah had left, I needed a room to move into. The rent for Bob's room was paid up for the month so I moved in.

That night, the storms broke. I watched, helpless, as the rivers of water ran through the streets and eventually broke through

the front door of my newly acquired accommodation. It was relentless but it only
lasted one night. As I waded through the
puddled floor, reminiscent of my first season's accommodation and left the apartment, I hoped that there would still be a job
for me on the beach.

I arrived at a scene of utter devastation. The
sunbeds had all been washed out to sea but
some were retrievable. I managed to pull
them from the water and arranged them
in a fashion that resembled the normal. As
soon as the storm had arrived it passed, but
it had left a trail of destruction in its wake.
I took a shovel and proceeded to dig chan-
nels in the sand to allow the flooded beach
to drain into the sea.

As the sun started to burn through the
clouds, the tourists came down to the
beach and the day-trippers arrived in the
boats from Rhodes. The crossing hadn't
been kind in that the waters were still un-

settled and the trip had been choppy. A few of the day-trippers were glad of a sunbed to lay on and when the sun finally broke the beds soon filled up. I sold them at a reduced rate as it was already well into the afternoon. When I took the days takings to Dimitris he was astonished as he hadn't expected me to sell a single bed. As I handed him the money, which was just less than what I was normally paid he handed the entire amount back to me. I took that as a sign that he trusted me.

For me, the saddest thing about this storm was that some people had lost their lives as a result. A transfer coach had attempted to make its way from Rhodes Airport to its final destination and such was the force of the water cascading down from the mountains on its route that the coach was washed off the road and down into a deep ditch whereupon many of the passengers were killed. It's difficult to imagine a scenario where you innocently take a holiday abroad but never return.

Fittingly, there is a roadside memorial in tribute to those unfortunate few.

The season had ended and I was in a quandary. I had reached a crossroads in my life and wasn't sure which turning to take. Sarah had left but I felt sure there was still something between us. We had exchanged contact details so I decided to travel home again. I packed everything I had which filled four suitcases. On mums various visits she had bought me an extra suitcase as I had only travelled light originally. I had everything. My tools, my clothes, my CD player, all my CDs, all my cassette tapes, all my unwashed underwear.

I had an unsavoury experience as I landed at Athens airport for a connecting flight. I had been out of the UK and in Greece for too long and I had aroused suspicion. I had my suitcases opened at Athens Airport by customs officials and they probably wished they hadn't. They had to witness the sight and smell of my unwashed underwear. I felt sure that my time in Lindos was done. I had said a few goodbyes to the people that mattered to me and I paid a last visit to Lindos Gardens.

It was derelict. It had been built in the shadow of some extremely tall mountains and rock faces and the sheer weight and force of water cascading down had mercilessly unleashed its destruction. I felt an equal measure of karma and sorrow. I had loved working there and I hoped that Vassilis would recover from this.

Sarah came to see me when I got home and I paid her a reciprocal visit to where she had relocated. It was clear that there was nothing more between us and she had decided to move on with her life. When I look back now I realise we were probably incompatible. We had very different needs and goals and hers were greater than mine. My goals were less surmountable and were really only pipe dreams.

I kept in touch with Rena and Cliff who informed me that Bob was planning to return for the 1995 season and gave me his contact details. We travelled back together from Gatwick to Athens and then took an internal flight from Athens to Rhodes. I had repacked all my stuff into fewer suitcases but the distribution of weight meant that my suitcases were considerably heavier individually than when I had last travelled with them. The initial flight was on time but for some reason, connecting flights were via a taxi transfer even though it was from the same airport. Our luggage took an absolute eternity to come through and one of my cases was the last to appear. It has to be someone and this time it was me. We got caught in heavy traffic and missed our connecting flight.

I'm happy to say that we spent the night in Athens airport waiting for the early flight in the morning and we made use of the 24-hour bar facility. I'm less happy to say that Cliff was waiting for us at Rhodes airport to take us back to Archangelos where we would have a slap-up dinner at a chicken restaurant and that sadly we wouldn't make it. We would get there eventually, later in the season, but the Greek Gods had frowned upon us that night. In any case, I was back. It was preseason but I had no job and no prospects.

I had muddled around and found some work but I was bored. The season was still months away so I decided to go island hopping. I took a slow boat from Mandraki Harbour in Rhodes and visited Symi, Kos and a few other islands such as Tilos. I spent a few nights on Symi and it was a worthwhile trip. I was surprised to learn that a boat crossing to Symi cost considerably less than the Thomson reps had been punting it out at during all those welcome meetings. It proved to be a productive trip as I had the opportunity to practise the Greek that I had been learning. By this time I could also read Greek and although I couldn't decipher an entire sentence, I knew a lot of keywords. I stopped at a hotel in Kos, which was expensive per night but when I tried to take a shower and realised it was ice cold I decided to investigate the fuse board in the room. I found one trip switch that had been turned off and it was marked *thermosifonos.* I knew this was the Greek word for *water heater* as I had replaced many water heaters in Lindos so I flicked the trip switch on, waited for an hour and had the best hot shower. A little knowledge is power.

I returned to Lindos with no clear game plan ahead. I wanted to work for Cliff again but needed a new direction. I found the usual preseason work repairing things and getting rooms ready which suited me. I didn't need to work every day of the week and I was starting to appreciate how the Greeks work hard all year and then enjoy a Winter of relaxation. All of a sudden I got some life-changing news. That sounds a bit dramatic. It was, but don't hold your breath.

Chapter Six

Season Four: The Summer of 95

I knew of Jake, a little. Our paths had never really crossed but I knew he was the sunbed king. He had gone back to the UK for personal reasons and had left a situation vacant. Dimitris had moved his sunbed business from Pallas beach to a larger beach on the other side of the bay of Lindos and there was the opportunity to work for him again. This was the year that the traditional style of metal fold up sunbeds had been demoted for scrap metal and a new swanky white plastic sunbed had turned up and was dubbed the new kid in town. The larger beach was divided up into many sections, all owned by various people and they had invested a lot of money in these sunbeds.

Jake's job had always been to put the old sunbeds out in the morning and collect them at night, locking them away. There was a new urgency now though as Jake wasn't here anymore and they needed someone who could put these beds out in the morning and put them away at night.

It was hard work as always, but I accepted the challenge like a boss. I was responsible for putting out five sections of beds at 60 beds per section, and then I would look after Dimitris' sunbeds all day, as I had done the previous year but without the privilege of having a second job running concurrently.

It was a no brainer though. I was paid 2000 drachmas each for the four sections and a further 5000 drachmas from Dimitris so I am earning the ridiculous amount of 13000 drachmas a day. This was precious money in the 90s and it was more than you could spend in a day. I soon started saving money again, and Dimitris would top up my wages with the profits of the bed resales. Dimitris was also responsible for a money exchange in the village, and I would regularly convert my wealth into sterling and send it home to the UK with friends who had come out to visit, entirely trusting them to pay it into my UK bank account.

My test of allegiance with Dimitris would come later that year.

I wasn't prepared for the complications that would arise from the simple task of being a sunbed attendant though.

The owners of the individual sections were territorial and out to make as much money as they could. I was situated at the far end of the beach and was sandwiched between two sunbed owners that hated each other.

Sunbed business is very different nowadays in that you can freely walk onto a beach and pitch up on a sunbed. Someone will eventually come to collect the rent but if they don't then you just managed to acquire yourself some free accommodation for a few hours.

It was very competitive back then and it was all driven by money. Each owner was very protective of their patch and would aim to sell and resell as many beds per day as possible.

It wasn't really my thing but we would *catch* people as they walked onto the beach and frogmarch them to the nearest available bed, irrespective of where they wanted to sit or lay and we would take their money. If I let a potential customer go to my right I would get verbal grief from my left and vice versa. Looking back now, I hated it

I learnt how to say, "would you like sunbeds?" in another four languages and when asked, "how much?" I would reply with the current price in their native language.

I more than impressed myself some days, as I could also use my four new languages to ask them if they wanted to sit near the water or to the left or the right or wherever but I didn't really care for these ridiculous wars the section owners got themselves into over a patch of fucking sand for fuck's sake. I would choose to use my own discretion at times.

There was an instance one day whereupon I had mistakenly *stolen* some customers from the section to my left. A young couple had walked down to the beach and I had two free sunbeds directly adjacent to another two which belonged to the next section. I freely offered them the choice of either my sunbeds or the adjacent two in the next section and they chose mine, not for any particular reason. At this point, the owner of the section came running down the beach, accusing me of stealing his customers. I clearly recall what I said.

Take your fucking customers, take your fucking money, I said, as I offered my customers the option to move

Unfortunately, he had only understood the expletive part of that sentence and had thought that I'd told him to *fuck off.*

He raced back up the beach in fury and spent 1000 drachmas on a phone card from the beach kiosk so he could call The Police and report me for stealing his business. This was utterly inexplicable behaviour as not only had he lost the sale of his sunbeds but he had also spent almost the same amount on a phone card and doubled his losses.

It was much later on in the season, but a young attractive girl had turned up on the beach one day, alone, and sat herself down on a sunbed. The pricing structure was ridiculous. It was 1200 drachmas for two beds with an umbrella but if you just wanted a bed and umbrella it was 1000 drachmas. I went over to collect her money, and when she enquired how much it would be, I explained the list of charges. She wasn't English and I couldn't quite work out if she was German or Scandinavian but she spoke fantastic English with that delicious accent that only a well educated European can.

"So if I don't want an umbrella it's only 600 drachmas?", she asked.

"If I leave you all day in the sun, you are either going to get burnt or you'll suffer heatstroke", I advised her. It was late July/early August, the temperature was around 38 degrees or more and the only other shade on my section of the beach was a big tree that I used to sit under with a wooden table and my book of tickets. I took a spare sunbed off the beach that had just been vacated and dusted it off and pulled it into the shade of the tree.

"Take this one", I offered her, "and just pull it into the sun when you need to".

"How much?", she asked.

I figured that Dimitris could afford to lose the resale of one bed and if I got *found out* I would have reimbursed him

"This one is on me", I said and she smiled sweetly in gratitude.

After a few hours, she came up and sat with me in my office and we chatted and smoked a few cigarettes together. It turned out she was just island hopping and was due to leave in the morning. She asked me out for a drink later on the evening, which I did, and we went on to have a meal together in a restaurant, for which we paid our equal share. She was amazing company, and although I found her extremely attractive I respected the possibility that she may have just been looking for company and nothing else. Sometimes, the memories of a pleasant evening can be jarred by the un-pleasantries of a drunken fumbled shag. I escorted her to her apartment to make sure she had got home safely and then went out to have a drink. Probably.

I would live in many different accommo-dations this year varying from the sublime to the ridiculous. Thankfully it would start with the ridiculous and then to the sublime and then regress to something more medi-ocre. But a man's kingdom is his home, and I was thankful for anything or anywhere to put my head down at night.

I had got fed up with sharing rooms in the past and vowed this wouldn't happen any-more. I took on a room in a villa which was only really suitable for workers. I had only been there a month or so when it became apparent why. The drainage from the bath-room was slow and after a month of living there, the foul smells of the drains would fill the rooms. I spoke to the landlord who called a plumber. The plumber explained to me that this was his annual contract. The rooms were vacant in the winter and this would give the trees that surrounded the villa a chance to extend their roots into the waste pipes and eventually block them. I took my chance to seek accommodation elsewhere but I felt I couldn't leave my fellow renters, despite the fact they were all Australian and this was probably normal for them.

I found another place in the village which was far superior and I moved them all in with me. The monthly rental price was fair but, as I was the only person who had a room to myself, I agreed to pay my share of the rent pro-rata. It was quite expensive but I could afford it as I was already coining it in from my multiple sunbed business.

Some of the Aussies decided that they couldn't find enough work to afford their share, and considering they were sharing two to a room I wondered how much money they had come with and what sort of life they were expecting, although it wouldn't have been too different from my initial expectations when I had first landed in Lindos

With the rooms being evacuated and not re-let it was time to get out so I didn't have to subsidise the empty rooms. I found a lovely villa at the top end of the village. There were a couple of shared rooms which were occupied by four young female workers, two each to a room, and there was me on my own in the most spacious room in the villa. We had a shared bathroom, but the kitchen was pretty good, even by Greek standards. I will state, at this point, that I wasn't even slightly interested in my four female housemates. They were far too young for me and I would often meet them in the courtyard of our villa as I was leaving for the beach in the morning just as they were returning home from their nighttime jobs in the clubs. Can you imagine?

My sunbed job was fairly straightforward.

Get up at 5 am

Have cereal for breakfast.

Perform ablutions.

Walk/run down to the beach and put out 300 sunbeds in one hour.

Walk/run back to the room and cook a full English breakfast.

Go back down to the beach.

Spend the day on the beach arguing with the adjacent muppets.

Spend another hour at the end of the day putting away 300 sunbeds.

Go back to Dimitri and get paid with performance-related bonuses.

By this time I would have already earned

somewhere between 13,000 and 15,000 drachmas, but I was back home by 8 pm most evenings and I was bored so I started looking for evening work.

It was just before this that I thought I could do with a little break. I'd made good money so far that season and I was building up a big reserve pot. I made the decision, inversely, to go back to the UK, or more specifically, to go home for a week or so for a holiday. England was enjoying something of a heatwave at the time so I asked permission from Dimitris and he agreed to let me go if I could find someone to cover for me, and so I did.

The break was more than welcome. It wasn't anywhere nearly as hot as the temperatures I had acclimatised to, but it was still the time of year when the days were long and the evenings were warm. I had a week away, catching up with a few old drinking mates before deciding to return.

They had become more interested in my stories about my life abroad, and most likely thankful that I wasn't crying over failed relationships.

Normally, on a return journey it would be in the off-season months and I would be looking for work but I already had a job, so when I returned, I decided to lie low for a few days, just to enjoy a few extra days before I went back to work.

When I eventually decided to show my face again, Dimitris was more than relieved to see me.

Each sunbed section on the beach was permitted 60 sunbeds, to be sold at 600 drachmas each with the use of an umbrella, therefore 1200 drachmas for two sunbeds and one umbrella. If you filled your section you would make 36,000 drachmas a day, so after my wages, Dimitris is taking 31,000 drachmas a day. I'm not the boss, I'm just an operative. He makes more than me but it's his business.

The person I had chosen to stand in for me was something of a rogue though. This was high season and beds were sold and resold throughout the day. A sunbed could be occupied three times a day and would get a 100% resale value every time, therefore increasing the day's takings.

Every day, my deputy would be selling and reselling beds but after his days work, he would be handing over exactly 36,000 drachmas to Dimitris, getting paid his 5000 drachmas, but pocketing all the profits. Dimitris had become suspicious as he knew the beach was busy so he asked my adversary to the right upon which he was informed that many beds had been resold during the day.

Dimitris and I had mutual respect. I knew that he couldn't do this job without me but

I also knew that he trusted me and this was why he would give me bonuses on my busier days.

I let him down just twice in my employment with him. The first time wasn't my fault but the second time most definitely was.

Tax evasion was massive in the 90s and probably, no definitely, contributed to the downfall of the Greek Economy.

I was supposed to issue a ticket for each sunbed rented, which I did, religiously, and each ticket would have a date stamp on it, but it was one of those old rubber stamp things that you had to manually adjust every day and press into an ink pad.

The trick, and it was a trick employed by all the sunbed operatives, was that you would lightly stamp the tickets and then gather them up at the end of the day and reuse them the following day but placing a heavier date stamp over the top to obscure the initial date. It was a novel idea and it would be a 50% tax saving. Genius, but also illegal.

The Greek Tax Police were onto this and all the various other illicit practices that were going on and would turn up unannounced. In the UK, you would expect a government official or tax inspector to be smartly dressed and carrying a clipboard or a briefcase but not so here.

The tax inspectors would arrive in the main square of Lindos, often dressed in holiday clothes and sporting an *I Love Rhodes* hat and then proceed to the first business to check their books. By the time this happened, the phones would be ringing like mad throughout the village and all the business owners would be running around like headless chickens trying to get their affairs in order.

This happened to me.

It was early in the morning, the beds were out and I was taking money from my first few customers of the day. As I walked back up the beach to my rudimentary office I noticed someone at my desk going through my book of receipts and I just knew I was fucked. I had been caught out, just for obeying directives, but I was still working illegally so had no defence to present. I walked along the main beach and shouted the word that no Greek businessman ever wants to hear to each section. The Greek word for *Tax Police*. I watched as they ran to their sections and pulled all the duplicated tickets from the umbrellas and replaced them with legitimate ones.

I was at the wrong end of the beach and in the wrong place at the wrong time. It wasn't really my fault but Dimitris did get fined.

I got a little job DJing in a bar that has long since closed down now but it was fun. I didn't even want to be paid for this work. I was happy to stand behind a bar at a DJ desk and, equipped with the CD player that my sister had brought me out the previous year, and not to mention all the CDs that I had with me, I could produce a great mix of music across the evening. I love music of all genres and I think that DJs should sometimes use a little more imagination, diversify a little and play a few more off the wall songs.

My life these days sees me playing drums in a band regularly and I am so happy when we get asked to perform at a private function such as a wedding or a Big Number Birthday celebration. Party DJs are a waste of money and are completely overpaid for what they do.

Do you remember back in the 70s when we went to school discos and it was all set up on the school assembly stage and the DJ had a set of twin turntable decks, a shitload of flashing lights and a table at the back racked high with vinyl?

Can you really imagine how much effort that would have taken to set up and sound-check beforehand, not the mention the size of van that would have been needed to transport that amount of gear?

These days you only need a laptop, a high wattage PA and a digital music collection. And a Nissan Micra.

But I've slipped off on a tangent again.

The English girlfriend of the Greek bar owner was on breakfast duty and she would cook me breakfast in the morning and allow me to take a shitload of ice from their machine which I would pour into my all day flask to keep my lemon squash cool. I would also visit a local supermarket that would make me a foot-long ham and cheese batten sandwich at cost price which would have been about 60 drachmas (probably about 25p at the time) and I could make this last all day.

She was an amazing girl and I loved her to bits. She had a fun personality and a joie de vivre to boot. A fantastic friend as well.

My test of allegiance with Dimitris was just about to be tested one more time. I had finished my unpaid shift as a DJ, and, for whatever reason, I decided on going out clubbing, despite the fact I would have to get up at 5 am.

I met a girl in The Acropolis Disco – that was just the business name, there wasn't actually a disco in the ancient Acropolis of Lindos - and we hit it off. I had this random notion that I would like to make love to a girl on the beach, on a sunbed, or wherever, and I had the perfect opportunity to execute this. As we left The Acropolis Disco and headed towards the beach, the light was already breaking and I was pissed beyond recognition. We both fumbled a little before I realised I had a job to do. I ushered her away, to her disgust and proceeded to put the sunbeds out. The action of this physical work only served to send the alcohol racing through my veins and by the time I'd finished putting the sunbeds out I could feel myself physically retching.

I looked around and the girl was nowhere to be seen but I decided at this point that I had more than overindulged and I had been awake for more than 24 hours. I decided to stagger back to my room and sleep it off.

In the 90s, to own a sunbed business meant that you would have befallen hard times and this was your only income, so, as such, it was a privilege.

Dimitris had succumbed to cancer or possibly diabetes and as a result, he'd had an amputation and had a prosthetic foot fitted... The reason why he needed someone to maintain his business was simply that he was physically unable to do it himself.

I woke up eventually, in the late afternoon, with the horrible realisation of what I'd done. Finally sobered up I made the sorry walk to the beach to scenes of utter devastation.

There were sunbeds everywhere, thrown into disarray. The adjacent sections had already been cleaned up, stacked away, and locked up for the night.

When Dimitris realised that I hadn't turned up for work that day, he had been forced to go down and monitor his section in my absence. It was August and it was outrageously hot. I found a broken man sat under the tree and at the table that was loosely termed as my office.

"I'm sorry Boss", I started.

"Ela vrai Xhristos", he replied, the first time

he had ever spoken Greek to me.

"It's your choice. Either you want to work for me or you want to go out at night and fuck girls. But you can't do both".

I looked at him and could see he would take days to recover from this.

"I want to work for you", I replied with remorse.

"Ok, are you going to close the beds for me tonight?", he asked.

I nodded.

He took 2000 drachmas from his pocket and paid me for my work at each end of the day. I vowed I would never let him down again.

I went out that night to find the girl to see if I could make amends. I did find her, but in no uncertain terms, I was rebuffed. It seems not everyone gives you a second chance in life.

The girls in the other rooms moved out and again I'm tasked with the option of keeping the villa on or moving on. I spoke with the landlord of the property and he told me he had another room, just next door, and it was self-contained. He showed me to the room and it was a bit basic. It had a small room that doubled up as a toilet/shower room. I had to take my loo roll out of the room every time I had a shower as it would get sodden from the spray of the shower but the room itself was large and had a large platform bed known as a Lindian bed. It was a raised wooden structure with storage underneath and it was surrounded by rails and balustrades, akin to what you would find in modern-day decking structures. There was also a lone fridge in the corner but I had no cooking facilities. Phil, my *Greek tutor* lent me a three-ring camping/outside barbeque stove, but the problem was I had no surface to install it on. I had a word with Alecos, my landlord, and two days later he knocked on my door and presented me, with pride, a table he had constructed himself out of raw materials. It was basically an upcycled pallet but I was chuffed to bits. He'd either built and tested it on an uneven surface or the floor of my room was uneven but it wasn't completely stable and needed the addition of a wedge or two to stop it rocking. I often wondered what the girls I had bought back to my one room apartment thought of my living standards. It was always clean and tidy – just in case – but it must have looked pretty appalling by their usual standards. Perhaps they were too drunk to notice or cast dispersion?

My room was complete, but who was I kidding?

I still had a perfectly useable bedroom in my parents' house with the addition of all the home comforts such as a hot meal every night cooked by mum. I started to wonder if I was cut out for this basic living.

Possibly the worst thing about this room was that it had an opening in the wall but there was no glass in the window neither by default nor design. The only thing that would keep the room cool during the day was to close the shutters and the only thing behind the shutters were four steel bars cemented into the opening. I had, in reality, rented a prison cell.

But I loved this room! I eventually learned to sleep through the sound of the donkey hooves making their way down to the donkey station in the morning.

September was approaching and I was looking forward to it. The days become shorter and the beach empties sooner and so the sunbeds are packed up and put away much earlier. This gives me a chance to socialise more with the September regular holidaymakers, and, by this time, I have managed to fall out with the owner of the bar that I was DJing for free. It mattered not to me as I removed my equipment and my stack of CDS and just sort of left him to it.

September is bittersweet though because you have the best weather in terms of it being finally manageable and it's a month-long frenzy of all your friends coming back for their second holiday of the year. If you had any sense you would get on the first plane home after the 30th of September. The problem is you don't because there is still another month of the season left and you feel it still has something to give, but it disappoints every time. The weather is ok but the village quietens down dramatically and runs on about 50% of its normal activity. It's a wonderful time to catch up with friends and get out socially instead of working for a living so ideally when October is put to bed, you should pack up your things and go home for the Winter.

But you don't, or I didn't anyway. November in Lindos is glorious. The sun shines every day and the village is calm. It's akin to a tinnitus sufferer who has a day of respite. No rooftop extractor fans are running anymore as the restaurants are all closed down and there is generally no buzz of activity....no electrical hum, or no electrical wow that you would associate with a normal season. The bars stop pumping out music at just after midnight and you get a real sense of calm instead of the manic existence you had grown to accept as normal.

November passed and I decided it was time to leave and make a brief stop at home. I had reached a crossroads in my life once more. I had sent a lot of money home with various visiting friends but I still had around three thousand pounds in sterling which I had exchanged with my boss and mentor Dimitris. I don't want to brag here but I had a similar amount already waiting for me in a bank account in the UK so I felt cash-rich for the winter. I felt I had finally beaten the Greek system of paying English workers a pittance for long hours. I had made a profit and it seemed a far cry from the days of digging out a cesspit and shooing away the irritating little buzzy insects as I did so.

I was ready to leave Lindos, but not ready to give up a life in the sun. I needed a new direction, a new venture, and a different country to achieve this.

My previous visits back home in the winter months had been a challenge. The first thing I would notice would be catching your breath as you stepped off the plane and the temperature would be *at least* twenty degrees lower than you had been used to.

I had left the UK some years before and I wanted some more time in the sun and in a foreign country before I could make up my mind about my future.

I hadn't really travelled outside of the English coastline too many times in my life. I grew up in the 1970s and family foreign holidays weren't an option back then as families didn't have money, so annual holidays were restricted to what was on offer in the UK. Mum and dad took me and my two brothers and my sister to some fantastic resorts though. We saw a lot of the Butlins holiday camps and a few Pontins as well. It was adequate enough for four kids who had no expectations of anything higher.

I was the eldest, my immediate brother and sister were twins, - the brother and sister that had been out to see me - and there was a younger brother. There were only four years between myself and the younger brother and we all had birthdays at the latter end of the year so it's fairly obvious how our parents kept themselves warm in the winter months.

My younger brother had managed to by-pass all the ugly genes that myself and my twin siblings had managed to take on. I don't mean that in a nasty way as, in fairness, we have all aged well and don't exhibit that outward appearance of being in our fifties, but Martin was a good looking boy. He had a different sort of cuteness as a baby and an infant and he developed into something of a pinup as he got into his late teens. He worked as a lifeguard at an outdoor swimming pool and he was regularly bronzed with sun-bleached hair. Is this relevant to this book? It will be later.

I had been on a school exchange trip to France when I was in secondary school. That would have been my first trip outside of the English coastline. I stayed with a family in Vesoul and it was in the height of the French summer which would have been about the same time as ours, as we are only a few miles apart. It was a glorious time by comparison to my exchange friend's trip to the UK whereupon it pissed down for two weeks. He was a wimpy little twat and allergic to a lot of things, which became apparent as he spent most of his stay with a runny nose.

His parents were obviously wealthier than mine as we holidayed for a weekend in their caravan, something which my parents would never have been able to afford.

I was a model student regarding French lessons at school. I spoke it almost fluently and could read and translate any text with ease. This would possibly explain my ability to pick up languages later in life and my ability to absorb everything I would hear.

We had been on a school outing one day on the French exchange and I was bursting for a piss. I walked up to the front of the bus and politely asked my French tutor – he was my French tutor in school and was English – if the driver could stop the bus so I could go to the toilet. I had never had cause to use that phrase and as such hadn't been taught it. My French tutor leaned forward and said to the French bus driver, "Monsieur, il veut pisser". I was always keen to learn different ways in which to speak French and absorbed this unusual turn of phrase.

A couple of days later, I was sitting in a science class in a French school understanding nothing of what was going on. I wasn't advanced enough in the French language to be able to translate The Periodic Table and I was getting bored and I needed to piss so I put my hand up. "Oui?", the French teacher enquired. "Madame, je veux pisser".

The whole room went quiet and she looked shocked. She glanced her eyes towards the door. As I left and went to have a piss, I realised that I had probably used a French word in a French school that I wouldn't use as an English word in an English school. Perhaps I should have just said *Je veux aller au toilettes* which is most likely what I would have learnt in French lessons.

The reason I needed to piss was I had been drinking. Yes. Alcohol. I am 14 years old, no more than that, and this is the early eighties. There was a supermarket, the name of which I clearly recall.

Prisunic. I can still remember the advertising jingle that was played on a loop over the PA system in the store.

I had to Google this but they were still around in 2003 until they closed down.

A litre bottle of Krönenburg was cheap, probably around 10p in English money and you would not have been age checked back then, much in the same way you could still go to newsagents and buy cigarettes for your parents. I would get bored with being in a French school and disappear just after lunchtime and go to the supermarket and buy a bottle of beer. And drink it. I'm sort of ashamed of that now but maybe it would explain my future penchant for alcohol.

Is this relevant to the book? Probably not, but it would be a full eight years before I would get the chance to go abroad again.

C hapter Seven
Winter 1995

My only previous holiday time abroad before Lindos was a two-week break in Lanzarote in 1988. It was a fairly drunken affair with a couple of mates and I never bothered to go back. Everyone has a resort they will go to for the first time and decide that is their forever holiday destination but this wasn't the case for me. I knew that The Balearics enjoyed good weather all year round, so with a few thousand pounds in my pocket, I decided to go to the other island that everyone seems to like.

Tenerife.

I bought an open return ticket for four weeks, fully expecting to throw away the return ticket and make a new life in Tenerife. How different to Lindos could it be? It would have English workers, bars and jobs galore, and good weather.

The first person I met as I wandered through the town that evening was Roland, the Belgian guy that I had worked with at the early stages of Jacks bar construction. We were equally shocked to see each other.

I ended up sharing a 3 bedroom apartment with two French blokes. Alain spoke perfect English but Fabrice didn't. I used my French knowledge to converse with Fabrice and I spoke English with Alain. Alain had an English girlfriend whose name I don't remember, but she was most certainly on a lot of drugs. She wasn't even that attractive and I wondered what he saw in her as he was a reasonably good looking bloke and could have had his pick of women. She would spend most of the day in the apartment edging from being fast asleep to being barely awake.

Fabrice had this sort of street trader business going on whereupon he would sell necklaces.... ok this is going to take some explaining here.

He had a bag of normal uncooked rice and a really fine point marker pen. Under the scrutiny of a magnifying glass and with an extremely steady hand, he could write your name on this grain of rice and then enclose it in a small glass capsule of liquid which would magnify the writing. He would then put this capsule on a chain and it would become a trinket, or an identity necklace, apart from the fact that you couldn't really get a full name or date of birth on the grain of rice, so it was a shit idea. He asked me to come and work with him as he didn't speak English and he hoped I could attract some English punters but street trading was illegal and we were forever packing up the stall and running.

Votre nom sur un grain de riz.

If you consider the potential wealth in this it was a winner. I have no idea how many grains of rice there are in a supermarket packet but it must amount to thousands. I don't even remember what we were selling these trinkets for but we would have been on a profit margin of at least ten thousand per cent.

The problem was we sold hardly any.

We made no money. I mean not a bean or even a grain of rice. It wasn't worth getting out of bed for.

It was a shit idea and I doubt it would have made it past first base in a Dragons Den scenario.

I came home after two weeks. I hated it there. I met very few English workers that weren't doing drugs. I hardly spoke to a local in all my time there and the ones I did speak to seemed hostile, probably not towards me directly but just to English people in general but who could blame them? We had invaded their island, built shabby chic properties all over it and built wall to wall and street to street bars. The great unwashed of society had cashed in their pensions or sold their own houses and moved abroad for a life in the sun, just because they had made friends with Pedro or Josè who had given them free drinks in the bar every night while they had holidayed there. They would get fucked over in years to come as they would have unwittingly bypassed planning permissions.

I found an English bar, which, in fairness, wasn't entirely difficult. The staff seemed friendly enough and I seemed to be welcome in there. Live music was frequent but the whole place was too English for me. Las Veronicas, another resort on the island, was a shithole and running wild with cockroaches wherever you went. I felt out of place there and didn't want to conform to that way of life.

It wasn't for me. I thought that living abroad was a generic thing but I was wrong. I was back home now but still unsettled. A quick Christmas and New Years Eve at home and I was booking a flight again. Back to Lindos.

I got some news that a local man was looking for a labourer for some building work. I would take anything in terms of work in return for a fair days pay. This was the first time I had really met Jack, not that one, but another Jack who was intending to turn his beach accommodation into a beach supermarket, and, actually, why not? The daily turnover would be a whole lot more than you could make just by renting rooms out.

This was bound to cause some upset on the

beach from the other business owners as they knew that Jack would be selling booze at supermarket prices which were at least fifty percent lower than bar and restaurant prices.

He was challenged one day by one of the beach business owners, asking him what sort of business he would be opening and what sort of products he would be selling.

I overheard this conversation taking most of it in until I heard the phrase

Isos poulíso profylaktiká

"Maybe I will sell condoms", was his reply.

He had certainly secured a corner of the market here as the beach was often an ideal scenario for late night/early morning activities but it was fascinating to me as I already knew that a condom is a prophylactic. So when we speak English every day of our lives we have no real idea that a lot of our language is derived from Greek and many other European languages. We just bastardise it or Anglicise it to suit ourselves.

We are an incredibly lazy race. We just expect that anywhere we go in the world on holiday that the locals will speak English. They usually do but if you are failing to be understood, just shout at them a bit louder, in English. That will always help. Something I learned was that when you speak to a local, it's always worth trying to gauge their grasp of English. Many Greeks are 75% fluent as they need to be but some are not. It was invaluable to me when learning how to speak Greek.

For example, and just to cite a really simple phrase, the Greek for *where are you from?* Is *apo pou eisai.* If you translate that literally back to English it reads as *from where you are?* That would be instrumental to me in understanding how the Greek language is structured, and to be able to differentiate between a Greek who could speak English and someone who was just repeating their own language with words they had learnt.

Jack explained to me that his right-hand man, Jake, was not available but I couldn't have cared less. Jack was a joy to work with and we had a lot of laughs although it was a freezing cold winter. Don't ever imagine a beach is somewhere you can go to and get your clothes off and sunbathe all year round because it can also be harsh and cruel, and when the cold winter winds blow in you have nowhere to go at the end of the day to warm up as your accommodation will be just a few degrees above that and your water heater will have exploded while you have been out for the day…..

I didn't actually finish the work with Jack as he informed me halfway through the build that Jake was coming back. I knew they were as thick as thieves and I didn't deny

Jake this work. I felt as though I had been a worthy stand-in in his absence.

C hapter Eight

Season Five: A New Direction

I'm back, and back to my usual preseason duties but I don't have any job sorted for the year ahead. Jake is back on the sunbeds again and my only option is to get up silly early and put out just 60 beds instead of 300 and take a massive wage cut. It's not really about the money though. The sunbed job sounds idyllic but it isn't. Aside from the competition from both flanks, it is exhausting to be working in temperatures of 40 degrees plus in high season for most of the day. I had got fairly used to the temperatures in peak season but I'd had an experience in the previous season that I will never forget.

When the sand gets hot it gets *really hot.* I had managed to acclimatise to this and I would patrol my patch of the beach bare-foot, whilst laughing at the tourists running across the sand, trying to dodge to the shaded parts.

I had just walked down to the front edge of the beach to collect money from my latest customers. It was around 2 pm and it was the hottest part of the day. I could feel the sand burning but not to a degree that it was bothering me. My world was just about to change. Someone had discarded a piece of chewing gum onto the sand, and I'm guessing that it had been there for at least an hour, nicely warming up.

When you have size 12 feet, they will naturally cover a larger surface area, but I guess this was more down to chance. I managed to step in the molten gum which could have been volcanic lava as the end results were not dissimilar. I felt the molten gum mould between my toes with such an intense heat that I could only hop back to my "office" and attempt to remove the substance. Despite the fact my feet had hardened and acclimatised, I had blisters between my toes for days.

I needed a new direction this year, however. I decided that I didn't want to do another year of sunbed duties and politely left Dimitris' employment. We parted amicably.

I hear on the grapevine that there is a job going on the beach. Not for Cliff and Rena though. I've known Mary and Mike for years but they aren't an English couple, as the names might suggest. Maria and Mikhalis Stadiatis. They have two children, Lefteris and Konstantina.

They used to have a fast-food joint on the beach just two doors from Cliff and Rena. They had decided to give up the business because, as Mary would tell me later, it was such hard work that when they finished for the evening, she would be so tired she would just fall asleep for hours and sleep on the premises for the night. I wonder now if that was an early sign of a condition that would take her life prematurely.

They had closed down the fast-food business and reopened it as a beach supermarket which would be challenging for many of the restaurant businesses, not to mention the fact that there was already another supermarket on the beach and was doing well. But times were changing. Tourism in Greece was suffering due to the extraordinary change in exchange rates and the fact that Greece was becoming more expensive in general. I witnessed a change in tourist behaviour. They were studying menus with more caution and they were watching their budgets. They would now be challenging Jack's Supermarket on the beach.

When Mary and Mike opened their new supermarket business, you could now buy a bottle of beer for a third of the price of a restaurant beer, you could get a filled roll for next to nothing, but you could also buy ice creams, hot and cold pasties, swimwear, sunglasses, chocolate bars, snorkels, cigarettes and spirits and so much more. I'm guessing that they wanted to make an easier life for themselves but they also needed to provide a bit of competition to try and undo some of Jack's business.

This was something I noticed happening frequently. If a particular business was doing well and another business just a few doors away was not doing so well, then over the winter the underperforming business would close, undergo a refurbishment, and reopen as a different business and it would be exactly the same business as the one that was thriving. I never understood this mentality, as in my mind, the only thing you properly achieve is to dilute the businesses and share the money.

My job was simple. All I had to do was to pick up the shop key from Mary's sister Tsambica, who had a longstanding supermarket business up in the village and make my way down to the beach. I would open the shop and move all the displays from inside the shop to outside, such as the hanging rails of swimwear, the racks of suntan lotion and the racks of sunglasses etcetera. I would then look after the shop for most of the day until Mary would come down at whatever time she chose and I would be free to socialise on the beach for a while. I would give her respite in the late afternoon while she took a siesta and then I would put everything back inside the shop at night. This job suited me. I would be thirty years old by the end of the year and while I realise that is still very young, I didn't have the stamina or enthusiasm to match some of the young workers who were turning up every year. I was settling into a way of life now. Besides anything else, I had Cliff and Rena two doors down, Theo and all his staff in Alex's Restaurant next door and Marianthi, Jack's mother, behind me in the Bouzouki Restaurant. I was surrounded by friends that I had made over the years and it felt like the ideal environment to be working, especially as it was less physical and stressful than operating a section of sunbeds.

I rarely saw Mike. He had a car hire and money exchange business in Lardos but he would make the occasional trip down the hill to the beach on his moped to deliver essential supplies. I never had full control of the shop in that I never had a set of keys, but I was expected to collect the keys by 8 am every day. It would take me all of five minutes between collecting the keys and getting myself down to the beach supermarket, and it would take me about 30 minutes to set it all up. Times had changed over the years. We wouldn't see a single tourist on the beach until 9 am at least.

Occasionally I would be out late and get back to my room later than I should have, knowing that it would be a struggle to get up in a few hours time. I had the most wonderful alarm clock and that was Mary and Tsambica's father, Kosta. He lived in the house next door to Tsambicas supermarket where I would collect the keys from. If I hadn't turned up by ten minutes past eight, he would jump on his motorbike and race round to my room on the donkey path and hammer on my door.

"Vrai Xhristos Malaka, dhoolea tora". Very basic but it would translate as "Chris, get to work now, wanker", and it would frighten me from my sleep.

I liked the easier days, but I would normally

be finished by 7 pm latest. My daily wages were considerably reduced when compared to just a year ago and I was surviving but I realised I probably needed a second job or one that would give me something to do in the evenings with the possible bonus of free drinks while I worked.

An opportunity was waiting around the corner, well, not so much as around the corner but on the same street as I lived. The same place that I had excavated rocks for the foundations all those years ago.

Jack had opened The Courtyard Bar the previous season although it was late into the season, September if I recall. I had been in a few times for the occasional drink after he had opened and it was pretty impressive. He had more or less built this place himself with the help of his father who had adorned it with his hand-painted plates and various other artefacts. I had always known Jack as something of a perfectionist and it was of no surprise to me that he would want to play a major part in building something that would be his lifelong ambition. He had been a local favourite in Lindos for decades and this would be his natural progression to be a successful businessman in his own right. With his fanbase and loyal customers of his beach restaurant, it was only natural that success would continue.

I had managed to retain my *palatial* accommodation from the previous year and would often stop in at The Courtyard of an evening.

Jack had built a DJ station that was up a flight of stairs and overlooked the bar and the dance floor. He had a young Greek local boy who was coming in to play music most nights of the week but, being young and Greek, he probably had more important things on his agenda and his attendance was erratic.

I offered to stand in for the young boy on his nights off and would often turn up just to see if he had bothered to attend that night. Eventually, I was hired as the resident DJ and I loved it. I had one small proviso which was that, as wages, Jack would pay me enough to cover my accommodation costs and I would never have to pay for a drink while I was working. It seemed to work well between us as my monthly rent was, by now, 60,000 drachmas per month which equated to about 2,000 a day and there wasn't a DJ in Lindos who would work for fours hours for that small amount, but then, neither did they have the penchant for alcohol, that I did. If you offer me unlimited drinks I will, or at least, I would abuse that privilege. I was quite high functional back then and could operate normally, even under the influence of alcohol. I guess we all did it, in whatever job we did, because we worked on adrenalin. The fact that I could empty the best part of a crate of Amstel bottles and smoke my way through an entire packet of cigarettes in a four-hour shift should have been a concern to me, but it wasn't.

I was still young and fit with an amazing capacity to recover quickly from any binge night out.

I had developed an illness, though. A condition. Its literal translation from Greek meant that I had herpes which is something you would normally associate with being an STD, although it turned to be something less sinister. I simply had shingles, a variant of chickenpox which is something you will inevitably catch as a child but will remain dormant until such a time as you are at a low ebb or will come into contact with someone who has had it or, more to the point, someone who has had contact with someone who has had it but will be asymptomatic.

I went to see the local doctor who informed me that my condition was treatable but expensive. I had other options though. The doctor, with all his professionalism, told me that if I had a good Greek friend locally, I could ask them to collect my prescription for the medication and they would only pay 25% of the cost. It was a no brainer. I could have flown home and got the medication free on the NHS but the opposing costs of a flight home caused me to seek local friendship.

It was a hard week. The doctor advised me that I *should* avoid alcohol as I was taking antibiotics so I did. I think he may have just been bullshitting me though. I survived that sorry experience and stayed sober for a week. The first drink after that never felt so good but, inversely, a week without alcohol and I was feeling a lot fitter and healthier. I was waking up in the morning with a clear head, often far too early and I had the chance to ponder on what the day ahead would bring. It was nice to be sober for at least a week. My brain was functioning normally again and I didn't feel the need to wake up and pour gallons of coffee down my neck.

I'm fairly sure that the worst thing about being teetotal is that when you wake in the morning, that is the best you'll feel all day, but I was clinically the opposite.

When you are young and can consume alcohol in large amounts daily you never class yourself as being an alcoholic but that was undoubtedly what I was.

Thankfully, that didn't last long and as soon as I was allowed off the leash, it was business as normal. I have an addictive trait. I don't know if it's inherited or even genetic but my Dad could never properly give up smoking and he always liked a drink, although Mum would often curtail his habits. My brother Martin was a hopeless drug addict but it's impossible to tell if that was just a result of the downfalls of experimenting with drugs.

I'll freely admit that I did have a drinking problem back then and the root cause of the problem was that I rarely had to pay for a drink, or not at full price at least. Outside of my usual employment, I frequented the bars that would give me cut-price or BOGOF arrangements or just those that would allow me to drink on a tab all night and then charge me a pittance when I came to settle up. The feeling of staggering home after a good night out, with or without someone in tow would be made all a bit sweeter knowing that it had probably only cost me less than 2000 drachmas. Or less than a fiver.

I found the transition hard when I would come home in the winter and two pints of beer in an English pub were costing me as much as a night out in Lindos.

It's 1996 and mobile phones haven't properly been invented yet. I wouldn't own my first ever mobile phone for another three years and when I did get one it wouldn't contain all the bolt-ons and apps that we are so familiar with these days. It had a poor LCD display that wouldn't even show the caller name, but just a number.

We didn't have mobile phones but we had a network of contacts. We all knew, at any time, where we all worked and for whom, and you could be contacted easily by phone.

I had, by this time, become known as something of a handyman or a general fixer of things. Everyone knew where to find me, and I would regularly get calls at the beach supermarket to come and fix something. Mary would always let me go without question and I would run up the hill from the beach to the village, grabbing my tool bag from my room en route. I would be back down within the hour having made some rudimentary repairs, or the simple action of flicking the trip switch on the fuse board to "ON". No need for an invoice in Lindos. That just involves the taxman so when asked "how much?", a reply with a simple "whatever you like", and an amount of cash would be handed over, and that amount of cash would almost double my days entire wages.

I was starting to think on a different level now. What if, and just what if, I could survive out here as a handyman or a general fixer. It would at least give me fewer working hours during the day and I could work the hours that suited me but still make money. I guess I had finally acquired some sort of status now. I was known to many as "Busy Chris", as I would often be seen running around the village, tool bag in hand.

Evripides had hired me to put up some new

signs outside his restaurant that he had made for him by someone or other. With my hammer drill to hand and a selection of rawlplugs and screws in my tool bag, it was an easy job and completed within less than an hour. My old sunbed *affendicos* (boss) had witnessed this entire event so when I was handed over the princely sum of 3000 drachmas for about an hours work he looked gobsmacked.

Vrai Xhristos, I pay the same for all day working on the beach.

I shrugged my shoulders as if to hint that skilled work is always paid better than manual labour.

I was contracted out to do similar work. Mikhalis, the local pharmacist, was moving from his tiny little shop to a brand spanking new pharmacy in the middle of the village. He'd had some rather nice painted signs made for him so he asked me if

I could install them at various locations around the village. It took me no more than a couple of hours and he paid me the unbelievable sum of 15000 drachmas. All I'd actually done was to drill a few holes in a few walls and insert some rawl plugs. My material outlay was minimal.

I'm really settling into my DJ job. I love music, always, have and always will. I have no real discrimination as far as music or genre is concerned. You would expect that an old man, as I am these days at the age of 54, I would be deeply rooted in the late 70s and early 80s. Not so. I still follow current chart artists and will occasionally download an album from iTunes. I do miss the excitement of going into a record shop and picking up an album and reading through the sleeve notes though.

If you could pin me down to a specific era it would still be the late 70s and early 80s and the bands that were inspirational to me, but more so, the drummers who influence my current style.

Clem Burke was my absolute hero, but that was more to do with the fact that I was a huge Blondie fan and had Debbie Harry posters all over my bedroom wall. Stewart Copeland of The Police, Gilson Lavis from Squeeze, Rick Buckler from The Jam or even Cedric Sharpley from Tubeway Army. All hugely individualistic styles but all very influential. It would be a few more years before I would appreciate the talent of John Bonham, Keith Moon or Ginger Baker, only because I had never properly been introduced to that era of music.

Perhaps the greatest drummer who ever lived and had a CV longer than any drummer could ever aspire to would be Hal Blaine, who performed on so many songs over the years but was never really credited or recognised. He was paid for his duties obviously but when you hear a song you love you never think about the musicians behind that song who provide the backing track. Of course, many musicians would fit that description and not just drummers. He played for Elvis, Sinatra, Simon & Garfunkel and just so many more. He was 90 years old when he died. I would love to have that legacy behind me.

I expect most of you will have skipped through the last page so I'll get back to reality.

The DJing job at The Courtyard is a winner though. Jack is always one step ahead of the competition. He has built a specific DJ booth on a raised platform that overlooks the dancefloor. He has supplied all the equipment and all the CDs and, to satisfy my undiagnosed OCD, they are all arranged in alphabetical order. Jack was moving into a new era though. The idea of having large stashes of vinyl records was becoming a bit passé and he had bought two CD players with which you could adjust speed control and pitch of the CDs, therefore you could effortlessly mix dance tracks, matching Beats Per Minute (BPMs). I could take this a level further though because as dance music is designed to be mixed, they all have similar BPMs and are often in the same key. Only the most discerning ear would know if your mix was a sixteenth of a beat out anyway.

I could mix anything from rock to reggae or punk and with such a wide choice of songs available to me, including my CD collection I had brought from home, I was spoilt for choice. Besides anything else, from my elevated platform, I had a full view of the dance floor, and I felt like the King of my Castle. There is something special about being a DJ. You can be responsible for controlling peoples emotions. You can make them happy and they will dance all night or you can throw in a song that will take them back to a specific moment in their life that they, and only they, will appreciate. It was never intentional. I would just find a random track that I wanted to play and I would somehow find a kindred spirit in the audience. It wouldn't be an uncommon sight to see a bottle of Amstel appearing at the top of the stairs just as a "thank you", and it was one more Amstel that would be a profit for Jack instead of a loss.

I'm happy to say, so far, these are the best years of my life in Lindos.

The UK beckons again. It was only a year since my last trip home in the season but this time is for a different reason. My sister is getting married and I'm not missing this for anything.

Nobody wants to read the details of a wedding of someone they don't even know so there's no need to include it here but my sister and future brother in law had chosen the date well. July 13th 1996 and, as per usual, it was a glorious English summer, something we aren't blessed with or guaranteed these days. It was a short trip and was over in the blink of an eye but I needed to get back to what was becoming reality for me.

There are so many stories of my time as a DJ I could recount but I had a rather more sedentary job as a supermarket operative which was equally enjoyable.

A whole life away from my previous year of sitting in the burning sun all day and fighting for beach space with two lifelong adversaries, I am now sitting in an air-conditioned shop, just dealing with customers and ringing money through the till. It was about this time I would get to meet Nikos. Nikos was working for Mary's husband Mike in the money exchange/car hire business in Lardos but he would come down to the beach supermarket to give Mary a little afternoon respite and to assist me in general.

Mary and Mike's son would finish school in the late afternoon and come down to the beach. He was a lovely lad, about eleven years old at the time, but, unlike his father who was fluent in English, and well versed in Italian, Lefteris was a bit lacking in the languages department so our conversations would be limited to Greek which was a massive help to me as I wanted to learn further. Unfortunately, most of our conversations would just have been me telling him off for something or other. He had this unique ability to destroy everything he touched, unwittingly or otherwise.

Next to the till was an ice cream freezer which was plugged into an extension lead as it was nowhere near a wall socket. This was one of those extension leads that had about four sockets on it with a master on/off switch. Lefteris had come down one day and while I was upstairs bringing drinks down to restock the fridges I had asked him to look after the shop. He knew how to work the till and could ring sales through and give the right change.

It transpired the following morning that he had inadvertently stepped on this master switch and turned the ice cream freezer off. By the time I opened the shop the following morning, the freezer was just a mass of unidentifiable fruity chocolatey liquid and wrappers.

It would frustrate me immensely. I was paid 5000 drachmas a day to open and close a shop and look after it all day, but by one simple act of clumsiness he could wipe out maybe 40,000 drachmas profit of stock with no recourse. He would come down to the beach to go swimming after school take a pair of trunks or shorts from the racks to wear, making them not fit for resale and at a cost of probably 2000 drachmas, this would have been two-fifths of my daily wage.

Nikos and I renamed him *Kyrios Katastrofi.* The Master of Disaster. It's perfect rhyming but I was learning more and more how so much of the English language is derived from Greek. *Katastrofi* = catastrophe.

This would be instrumental in something I would term as word association. For example, the Greek word for a plumber is *edhvraleekos.* Take out the middle bit, change the spelling a bit and you get "leak", which is something plumbers are normally hired to fix. Simple word association.

Here's another. I wanted to know what the Greek word for a fuse was or in modern-day terms, what we would now call a miniature circuit breaker. I was told that it was *asfalisi,* which translates as "insurance". Of course! Fuses and miniature circuit breakers are designed to protect and insure against life or death! This learning Greek lark is getting easier all the time.

Nikos and I remain friends to this day and who would have thought back then when we were just working together that I would eventually become a tourist and that he would open his own beach restaurant and I would become a regular customer of his beach restaurant?

The season pushes on and we have done the September element and we are now in the dregs of October. Much like the UK, we see the days getting considerably shorter and the night drawing in. The weather is unpredictable and it can be a lottery of whether it's glorious sunshine or all-day rain. One such day, I had been down and opened up the supermarket as usual and then the skies darkened and the heavens opened. By this time, the beach was half full and the customers were coming into the shop asking if we sold raincoats, as if we would.

Greece wasn't famous for bad weather so I had to think on my feet. We didn't have raincoats but we had a huge stock of bin liners so I cut a hole in the top and two slits in the side, and, hey presto, you have a waterproof mac. I sold our entire stock of bin bags that day at 200 drachmas each when we would normally sell a roll of ten for the same price. I turned off the till and rang no purchases through so it wouldn't show on the day's takings. Ever the businessman, I was always looking after my immediate employers. I think Mary was astonished at the level of money in the till but thankful she had a days business tax free.

October is now put to bed and I have a new opportunity on the horizon. An English lady is looking for someone to look after and maintain her property for the winter, rent-free and any expenses for any materials purchased to effect any repairs would be repaid.

Now I had properly landed on my feet. This was a real Greek Villa. Separate kitchen, bathroom, upstairs bedroom, huge living room with Lindian beds and a small black and white TV with an erratic reception. There was also a Video Cassette Recorder which in this day and age seems antiquated but we had no other options as Smart TVs and online streaming were yet to be invented.

October is done, November awaits and I'm still around. I'm not planning a Christmas in Lindos as I know there will be a Sunburnt Arms Reunion waiting for me in the UK. I'd already done a few of these which had ended in drunken disasters, often planning the night out but with no forward plan as to where I would sleep that night. I stayed with many unsuspecting people who probably took pity on me including Bob Penny, my Lost Boy counterpart Martin, and a random place in London where a young girl who I knew from the previous season had offered me a room at her place for the night.

I might just have thought that I was on a promise but the fact that I mildly threw up in the taxi on the way back and the fact that when we got back to her flat her boyfriend was already waiting up for her made me realise that the best option would be to find the nearest available soft furnishing and fall asleep.

I would often wake in the morning and wonder where the hell I was and how I would get home. Thankfully, I made it home and I'm still around to tell the tale.

So, 1996 is all done and dusted, various reunions done and sorted, Christmas and New Year with the family and I'm sorting out my sixth season. This time, I'm going away and I'm staying for good. I think I've finally found my forever home.

C hapter Nine

Season Six: A future awaits

I'm back again with no particular work planned for the interim months but at least my accommodation is free and I have a pot of money to survive with, regardless of what happens. I had arrived, full of excitement and I didn't really need to work as I could well afford not to.

Jack has opened the bar preseason, and he has done a few internal changes in the winter months. The upstairs DJ platform has now been moved under the stairs that I used to have to walk up and all the equipment and CDs have been moved, relocated and installed. I still have a job here, I didn't leave under a cloud, so it was good to have something to do in the evening, unpaid, but with free drinks.

I grew up in a mixed nationality family. I was born to an English mother and an Austrian father, as were my siblings, and we grew up with a diverse mix of music being played in the house. Mum and Dad had shared music tastes which would have included The Rolling Stones, Elvis Presley, Buddy Holly and many more but Dad also had an appreciation of other music which would include Italian and Greek and his native language of course. As a result, I grew up absorbing this music and, in time, I would learn to appreciate it.

Out of season, the bar would be mainly populated by the locals which would include the local Police. I'm not sure what rank they were but they held no high authority anyway. Let's just call them constables for ease of reference.

This would be a big move for me in a bid to learn a little more of the Greek language. I would mainly play Greek music in the bar in the winter months, but in truth, I had no idea what I was doing. I would just play any old song as long as I liked the sound of it. After a while, I was starting to get requests to play Greek music from the locals. I was a little bit scared as I didn't know a lot of Greek music but I would get asked for a particular song by a particular artist. Thankfully, Jack had aligned the CDs in alphabetical order so I would pull out the CD by the relevant artist. I would point to the back cover of the CD case and simply ask "Ti theleis?" meaning "what would you like?" and they would point to a song and I would play it. As my confidence grew, I would start to learn what songs they liked and would start to understand what they were asking for and could pull the relevant CD and song title and play it....to their delight. The Greek coppers loved a good Sambeccica dance. I'm not actually sure if that's how it's spelt but phonetically it's correct. It involved a lot of arm-waving, kneeling, and taking a shot glass from the dancefloor in the mouth without the use of hands and tipping it back and swallowing it.

It was entertaining for a while but the one thing that always astounded me was how the young Greek boys of the village, and by that I mean barely out of school, would favour songs by really old singers. They would find CDs belonging to Jack that looked like they were remastered from recordings made in the 1940s and they were really morose songs about love and betrayal and all sorts of nonsense. *Tragoudhia* was the genre and it just translated as *sad song* or *tragic song*. It would be the modern equivalent of a bumfluffed teenager preferring the music of Frank Ifield or Perry Como over Ed Sheeran or Jake Bugg, or whoever. Whatever the outcome, I am starting to learn the respect of the local coppers who would often buy me a beer in return for playing a song. That was priceless, and for me, it meant that I had finally proven to The Police that I was here to stay and the events of Winter 1992/3 could be put to bed.

The Winter season is nearly over, I've been doing a bit of DJ work to keep my hand in and I'm doing a little out of season work for Mary and Mike, cleaning and valeting their hire cars for the season ahead. I have two jobs, the same as the season before, so effectively, I'm settled. There's no reason whatsoever to go back to the UK now. I've done five, approaching six seasons already so surely this is me for the rest of my life?

Amazingly, I've now managed to keep my winter accommodation on. It was a good winter. I accommodated my old mate Robbo from Il Sogno -for free- he had a Playstation One with a handful of games.

We had got through the winter playing Resident Evil and Die Hard and mixed that in with the fact that we had a shit telly but a video recorder/player and I could play some of the VHS tapes I had bought with me which were mainly recordings of Harry Enfield and Paul Whitehouse. There was the occasional bit of soft porn on terrestrial TV as well if you wanted to find it but it was all a bit shit, to be honest.

It seemed I would at least have this accommodation for a little while longer but as per usual, it was about to go a bit Pete Tong.

I got short notice that my landlady, as I shall call her, had a friend who was coming over for a short stay and needed accommodation. Rob was staying rent-free with his latest girlfriend so I had to make the harsh decision to boot him out. He was fine about it and found somewhere pretty quickly. We had both enjoyed free accommodation for the winter anyway.

It was reported back to my landlady by her visiting friend that my gardening skills were less than satisfactory. I wouldn't describe it as a garden but just a load of things that had grown out of control in the winter in the courtyard, so I decided to cut them all back to practically nothing. I knew full well that they would grow back again but I was severely bollocked for my efforts.

I'd kept that place spotless and clean, I'd done some painting, repaired a major leak in the bathroom and most importantly it had been kept warm and dry during the winter. My only mistake was to get a bit over-exuberant with a set of garden shears. I'd had a good winter but I knew this accommodation wouldn't be suitable for the summer, especially as I would need more privacy if my landlady or any of her friends could turn up at a moments notice.

I found a fantastic apartment at the top of town. It was just over the road from the

Police Station but that didn't bother me. They had got bored of me by now and realised I was here to stay, and I had committed no 'crimes' since those early days. It had a double room, which I naturally commandeered, and a couple of smaller twin rooms. It had a good-sized kitchen and a shared bathroom, but it was light, airy, and clean. We had a cleaner who would come in most days and sort the place out save for doing any laundry for us but this mattered not as I had acquired a small washing machine from somewhere, and I really can't remember who I bought it from but it was a really small one, with a maximum wet load of about 3kg, so about half of what a normal domestic machine would cope with but it was adequate. I plumbed it into the cold water supply in the bathroom, which bizarrely had an electrical socket in it and connected the waste pipe over the edge of the bath. It worked brilliantly but water recycling in Lindos in the 90s was…….none existent. The wastewater would mainly get pumped out far into the Mediterranean but the prevailing currents would eventually bring it back into the bay of Lindos where there was no tide. In peak season you could see a film of oil and suds on the shoreline. I'm fairly sure that most of the holidaymakers were swimming with the contents of my underpants, but, as they were mostly Italian holidaymakers in August I won't lose any sleep over that.

Oh, that has just reminded me of something that happened in my first season. Rather than backtrack and edit the first chapter, I'll recall it here and now.

When I was working at The Pallas Taverna in 1992, a young lady came into the restaurant, asking if she could use our conveniences. We didn't have in house facilities but a dual WC block, behind the building and detached from it. Ideally, you had to be a customer to use the loos as, and this was inevitable, change of country, change of diet, excess of alcohol would mean that many customers would decorate the bowl with whatever had disagreed with them. If you were a paying customer it would justify that someone who was employed by Pallas Taverna would have to clean the toilets on a daily basis. If you are squirting someone else's product into our loos, you can go elsewhere.

I do remember the cleaning process though and it was quite fun. All that was needed was to empty the bin which contained the toilet paper and then outside the WC block was an outside tap with a length of hose attached to it. If you turn on the water supply to the hose and put your thumb over the end of the hose it will create a high-pressure jet, similar to modern-day jet washers. Who knew that the prototype Kärcher pressure washer may well have been inspired by a little old Greek lady hosing her courtyard down? So, no need to get your hands inside the toilet and remove the skid marks but just use the high-pressure hose to clean the entire room down, walls, floor, pan. Everything.

On this particular day, this young lady entered the kitchen area enquiring about the use of our facilities. Fast-forward thirty years to now and if Bob or Carolyn were faced with the same request they would have ushered this young lady to the toilets without protest but on this day they had the devil in them.

"Most people just have a slash in the sea", was Bob's deft reply and Carolyn backed him up. She left, not deflated but happy to take on the advice she had been given. They both watched as the young lady walked down the beach, eyeing the activity to her left and right. She finally walked into the water and after doing a peripheral check for the last time she squatted and relieved herself. Nothing wrong with that, you may ask, but at that precise moment, Bob and Carolyn witnessed the sight of a snorkel poking out of the water no more than a foot away from where she was pissing. I often wondered where those warm currents originated from in my future experiences of swimming in Rhodian waters.

Work in the beach supermarket was routine and predictable. It didn't vary much on a day to day basis apart from the occasional weird person who would come in with a strange request and I was still getting regular phone calls for odd jobs. There was a really bizarre incident when someone had turned up on holiday who was – clearly -a post-op transsexual.

I'm going to say *clearly but* in truth, she (?) was fairly convincing. It's important to remember that transsexuals were still fairly unheard of in the late 90s, and had she blended into the surroundings she would have remained inconspicuous, but she chose to perform outrageous acts such as taking naked showers on the beach when families were sitting nearby on sunbeds.

She came into the shop one day and Lefteris was sitting at the shop counter with me. She was wearing a pair of cut down denims which were unbuttoned and the fly was unzipped, revealing a full thatch of pubic hair.

Lefteris nudged me in shock. I had to ask her to leave but the news had got around the village and she was the subject of ridicule from all the local males wherever she went.

The DJing job had taken a new direction, however. When the bar had been remodelled in the previous winter and my DJ booth was now downstairs, I hoped it would put me on the same level as the customers and, hopefully, would create more eye contact, which would hopefully lead to more liaisons and conquests. This didn't seem to be happening this year, for whatever reason, and I was starting to re-evaluate my existence in Lindos. I did start to wonder if my decision to come back for another season was sensibly worth it until I got a phone call one morning. I didn't know it at that specific moment but it was a phone call that would set the seed of doubt in my mind. It would take a few weeks or months before I would act on that news.

It was a normal day. I had gone down to the beach and opened up as usual. On any other day, I would have left the shop wide open and gone for a coffee with Marianthi, Jack's mother. The beach rarely saw a customer before 9 am but today I just chose to sit in the shop and listen to the mixtapes I had compiled in the bar the night before. I was listening and admiring my skills as a DJ when suddenly the shop phone rang. There was no such thing as caller ID, so I swiped the slider volume switch on the cassette player down and picked up the phone.

Parakolo, I answered, not expecting it to be a call from anyone English at that time of the morning. We were two hours ahead of GMT.

Chris? Came the female reply, and then the line went silent for a few seconds. Eventually, the silence was broken and the voice of my brother in law came.

He was broken but more composed.

"It's about Martin", he started. I sat back in the chair and expected the worst news.

"He's tried to commit suicide by jumping off the top floor of a multi-storey carpark".

I took a moment to absorb this news myself before replying.

"Is he alive?", I asked.

"Just" was the short reply.

My next question was leading.

"Do mum and dad know?"

"No. They're away on holiday. If they call you for any reason please don't let on, we need to deal with this..."

I remember putting the phone down and leaving the shop wide open before going behind to see Marianthi. I knew that being of an older generation she would have been shocked at the news so I decided to withhold. I just said my usual cheery *kalimera* and she made me a coffee, as usual. I had been sitting in the restaurant for maybe an hour while collecting my thoughts when I was aware of a shouty voice.

Vrai Xhristos, ti kaneis edho? Magazi mou aneixai Kai lefta mou, ola mesa, giamoto?

For the uneducated, I will translate.

"Chris, mate, what are you doing here? My shop is open and all my money is inside for fuck's sake?"

I had the capacity to retort in Greek, but I couldn't be bothered, as I was still reeling.

Ela mazi mou, I replied, and we went to sit in the comfort of her shop. I racked my brains for a minute trying to explain my dilemma in Greek before I just decided to speak English, in staccato form.

"My brother. He try to kill himself yesterday. He go down. 20 metres. To concrete"

I saw the look in her eyes change, and her expression drop, as she realised I was now having to deal with personal grief, and she let me go for the day. Compassionate leave I suppose. I would surmise that it was about this time that my priorities would change, or if they hadn't done then, they would later that night.

I went to work as usual in the evening and divulged the news to Jack and Samantha. I agreed to carry on and work as usual as it would be a welcome distraction. About an hour into my shift, Samantha handed the bar phone to me and whispered, "It's your mum". In a flash of inspiration, I lined up Dire Straits' "Telegraph Road", and "Tunnel Of Love", to play back to back as this would give me around 21 minutes to engage my mum in a phone call.

She had made a random call. She and dad were on holiday somewhere, and she had just decided to call out of the blue for a catch-up. She had no idea what she would be facing when she and dad would get back home and it was the hardest phone call of my life as I had to act normal whilst knowing what was in store for them. They would have to return home and then go to see Martin laid in a hospital bed with wires and tubes coming out of him and his legs a broken mess. Incredibly he had survived, but more incredibly, he would walk again.

I probably realised at this point that I had served a purpose in Lindos and family values were far more important. I closed the call just as the incredible guitar solo by Mark Knopfler on Tunnel Of Love was playing out and resumed my duties for the evening.

I would wake the following morning as usual but I would view life from a different perspective. Just how long it would take to make the final definitive move was unknown at this point but I was just waiting for the right opportunity.

I started to realise that the age of the English who were coming out to work were getting younger and I was getting older. I was only just into my thirties at the time and looking back I suppose I was still a young man, it's just that I felt old. I felt I probably should have achieved more in my time there in terms of making some sort of successful life there or having forged a long term relationship with someone. I guess that would have been partly my fault as I preferred to just sleep around and change partners every couple of weeks.

I'd had the opportunity to make future successes of my two-week relationships as I would regularly receive letters in the Lindos Post Office, just addressed to DJ Chris, Courtyard Bar, Lindos, Rhodes, Greece, or indeed any of the places I had worked in over the previous seasons. I never bothered to reply to many of these letters, because......I didn't want to.

These days, if you mistype a digit on a postcode, Hermes will happily take it to a completely different county and throw it in the front garden without a care in the world, but if you just wrote: "Lindos, Rhodes, Greece", preceded by the name of the intended recipient your mail would always get there. We didn't have a postman who would deliver direct to your door, but everything just went to the Post Office and was separated into English and Greek piles. It would be a joy to leaf through the piles of letters and find something addressed to you.

This season had been particularly quiet in that respect and I think I probably had only three partners in the entire season, and probably the most bizarre thing about that now is I don't remember anything about them, not even a name or what they looked like. Perhaps I should have tried to answer some of those letters.

I had also stopped enjoying my jobs and that had nothing to do with my employers. I was compensating for the fact that I felt lonely and unhappy by drinking excessively, both in the evening at work and afterwards in the clubs, often until the small hours of the morning. I felt as though I was going backwards and everything that I had set out to achieve initially had been a waste of time. Kosta's hammering on my door was becoming more frequent, but I was only oversleeping due to the lack of sleep. I could manage the alcohol intake and recover easily from it but I was also smoking three packets of cigarettes a day and these were Peter Stuyvesant cigarettes which contained twenty five to a packet.

My diet was poor. I would snack on sandwiches, crisps and ice creams from the shop as it was part of my wages and my evening *meals* were usually burgers, pitta gyros or crêpes, mainly because it was fast and convenient and the drink and cigarettes were destroying my appetite, or at least my patience to sit down and eat something more substantial.

I've never been one to put on weight but I was now tipping the scales at somewhere between nine and ten stone. The strange thing is I didn't look underweight as I've always been, and still am, tall and slim but I was certainly undernourished. I guess those are the benefits of having a healthy golden tan for most of the year round.

These days I still struggle to get above eleven stone but my diet is much better and I put it down to my high metabolism. I'm resigned to the fact that I may always be this way.

I was tired, mentally and emotionally, but not physically. I could still do my work but I had become disheartened and disinterested.

It was mid-August, 1997, and the phone rang in the supermarket one morning. It was my sister. I hesitated but all was good. She was just phoning for a chat and a catch-up.

We spoke for ages about all sorts including how Martin was doing.

I then turned the conversation to Dave, my

brother in law and her husband, naturally. Dave had one of those old-style DIY shops in England, the sort that will sell you one screw from a box if that's all you want or will cut you a piece of timber of MDF to whatever size you want, or cut you a key, or a piece of glass or just about anything. These sort of places rarely exist now, including his shop.

I asked how business was, to which she told me that he was struggling, not with the business but with the staff and he needed a general manager to come in and help.

I jumped at the chance. I needed an exit strategy, an escape route, a reason to go home and start work. I didn't want to be an electrician again as I'd had so many years out of the trade I thought it would be difficult to get started again and I wasn't sure if I still had all my contacts.

"Tell him I'll do it", I replied.

"Really?", she sounded surprised.

"I need to get home Sue, this place is killing me".

She put Dave on, we had a brief chat, and it was all sorted. I had a job to go back to. It was just a case of telling Jack and Mary. I knew Jack would be fairly ok with it but I dreaded telling Mary. She was just one of the sweetest, loveliest people I ever worked for. She forgave me all my misdemeanours in my employment with her and I knew she would find me hard to replace as she trusted me implicitly. I could see her face drop as I broke the news and the final good-byes were difficult. I would learn later on subsequent visits as a holidaymaker again that she cried for days after that event.

She became increasingly unwell over the years that ensued and had to fly regularly to Athens for tests. I was shocked to see her one year when I came back and she was tubed up to an oxygen tank. She was only a few years older than me and she sadly lost her life a few years ago. I never got the chance to say goodbye a final time as I always believed she would get better.

For the first time in my life in Lindos, I was making final preparations to leave, permanently. I'm not stupid, and I realise that over twenty years later, it was of more importance to me than those that I would *leave behind,* but I had things to do, people to see, and a few bar tabs to settle.

I had *stuff* to sell. My washing machine, my Calor gas heater. I had *stuff* to get rid of. My daytime footwear had always been, for all my years there, a pair of leather sandals which were made locally and affectionately known as "Lindians". I wouldn't be seen dead in a pair of sandals these days, but these "Lindians" of mine were the best footwear I ever owned. They consisted of nothing more than a flat leather sole and a loop that you would slip your big toe into. I only wore them in the daytime. To wear a pair of sandals post-midnight when you've had a few drinks is just asking for a complicated walk home. I took them down to the beach and walked along the jetty to where the water sports and day trips operated from and launched them as far as I could throw them into the crisp Mediterranean waters. It was a sign that I had consigned my beloved footwear to a burial at sea and I had no intention of coming back. Sandals have something of a bad press. In my school days, anyone who wore sandals of any description was ridiculed for their open-toed footwear and the leather appendages were cruelly named as Jesus Boots. I'm going to state, for the record, that there is nothing healthier for the feet than wearing something without socks that allow your feet to breathe and form naturally. Our nation's obsession with wearing socks, trainers, winkle pickers, high heels and stilettos (for the girls) just force our feet and toes into unnatural positions and cause no end of podiatric problems such as athletes foot, bunions, ingrown toenails and all manner of things.

We just wear socks in this country because it's normally so fucking cold.

I booked my flight and prepared for my final night in Lindos. I treated myself to a proper meal in a restaurant for once and then went out and did my final goodbyes to all the bar owners. It was a pretty emotional time for me as, despite everything that was in store for me back home in terms of a job and a future, it was still an unknown quantity and an uncertain future. It could easily fail magnificently if I realised that I'd made the wrong decision and suddenly I would be back where I was six years ago, having achieved nothing save for a few irreplaceable memories.

The memories of that night are clouded now but I still remember waking up the following day, the day of my flight home, with the worst hangover in my history.

The only thing that I can clearly recall from that was my brief visit to Il Sogno Bar. I had been sat at the bar contemplating my future, when, without warning, Yianni lined up and played Spandau Ballet's *Only When You Leave*.

I know that Gary Kemp didn't write that song with my exit from Lindos in mind but on that final night, everything seemed so poignant and so relevant.

Only when you leave,

I need to love you.

And when the action has all gone,

I'm just a little fool enough to need you.

Fool enough too long.

I can never hear that song now without being taken back to those days and my final goodbyes.

Thankfully, my flight wasn't until the evening and I had the day to recover. I'd blagged a slot on one of the transfer buses to the airport and I'm finally on my way, for the last time.

I will return, but never to work there again.

C hapter Ten

Life after Lindos:

I left Lindos on what would prove to be a pivotal day in English history. It was August 31st 1997. I had arranged for my sister and brother in law to pick me up at Gatwick Airport. I had flown through the night and had arrived in the early hours of the morning. The usual painful transition of landing and retrieving luggage ensued and I walked out to arrivals to see the faces of two of the people I loved the most.

After an exchange of embraces, we walked towards the exit and the short stay carpark.

"Have you heard the latest?", my sister announced. I expected it to be the ongoing saga in my brother's struggle with drug addiction.

"What's Martin done now?", I asked, and, without wanting to sound uncaring, compared to what he had previously done, I wouldn't have been shocked at any reply.

"Princess Diana died last night, something to do with a car crash in Paris."

Back then there was no such phrase as *OMG* accompanied by a hand over the mouth but I'm sure my reaction would have been a predecessor to the modern-day equivalent.

We got into my brother in laws car and made the hour and a half journey home. There was a news blackout in respect of the fact that nothing was being reported other than updates and sombre music being played in the interim.

I have to say I was shocked as were many people in the immediate aftermath. I had no idea about what had happened and relied on the 24-hour news feed to keep me updated. The 31st of August would be pivotal for me, personally, but not for some years later.

I went to work for my brother in law as promised but I realised eventually it wasn't the job for me. I completely respect him for giving me the opportunity to start a new life in the UK again. Eventually, he would have to declare me as an employee and I was concerned that my unpaid tax affairs from the early 90s would catch up with me. Thankfully, I had been erased from all tax records and I was free to start being employed in the UK again. When I left his employment, I resumed my career as an electrician for a few years until I made a career move to become a kitchen fitter. This is a job I do to this day and one that I will most likely do until I retire.

Life was good again. I was back to earning good money as I had decided to go back down the route of self-employment. I was holidaying twice a year in Lindos although I found it difficult to behave like a tourist. My time there would be spent just visiting the same bars as I'd always done and going to the same beach. Despite having money in my pocket, I found it hard to get rid of. I guess one of the benefits of having relatively behaved myself during my time there was that I was more than welcome back and meals in restaurants were often half price and bar tabs were low, even though I was still managing to get through a sizeable volume of Amstel every night. I even slipped into my old shoes as a DJ and would often spend my evenings DJing for Jack, even though I was supposed to be on holiday.

Four years had passed by and I was still single. The "ladies" are easy to come by when you are tall, bleached blonde and healthily tanned, and I'll freely admit, it becomes a whole lot easier when you work abroad. Many female tourists, married, attached or otherwise just want the thrill of a one night stand or a holiday encounter with no further commitments or complications. That would be a reciprocal agreement for me.

As my last season in Lindos had been largely devoid of such chance encounters, my confidence with the opposite sex was waning again and I was finding it difficult to meet women once more. I had a brief relationship with a customer of mine but it was only about sex and very much on my terms. She had a key to my flat and would turn up on a whim and spend the night. Besides anything else, she had three kids ranging from 12 to 19 years old and I didn't want a ready-made family. She eventually got fed up with my lack of commitment, and I came home one day to find my key in an envelope on the desk in my small home office accompanied by a *fuck you* note. I took that as a sign that the relationship was over, and although, not completely phased by it, I did start to wonder if I would be a single man forever.

Many people often ask me how I met my wife. I'm not ashamed or embarrassed to say that these were the days before online dating, something we all think is normal now. We only had contact ads in the local newspapers at the time and they were expensive as you had to retrieve your messages by calling a premium rate number. You wouldn't get any form of notification that you had a message waiting so it would just be a case of periodically checking, often without any results. My phone bills were astronomical back then, and this was a landline and not a mobile number

I would always reply to any messages and meet up on blind dates, with varying degrees of success and disappointment. Some of the girls I met were stunning and way out of my league and others were just hor-rific. I'm sure they had nice personalities but this was a case of me being too good for the ugly girls again.

I met a lovely girl who lived about 15 miles away and we maintained a relationship for about nine months, albeit non-physical. I don't know why we never progressed to the next phase but the relationship just sort of died a natural death.

I decided to book myself another holiday in Lindos, not intending to go back to work there but maybe just to get laid again, as sordid as that sounds. I picked up a mes-sage in my "inbox" with a phone number to call back, to which I obliged. The call went to voicemail so I left a message. A short while later I got the call back which would shape my future. We chatted for a while and decided to meet up at a service station at a halfway point. We were geo-graphically close but I had no expectations at that point. She would later tell me that her first thoughts as I alighted from my car were that "if I shag that it will break". She wasn't a big girl but I was neither well built. Most blind dates up to this point had been decided, by me anyway, after the first few minutes but there was something mysterious about her. Something that I needed to know more about. She wore a white blouse and skin-tight jeans. Her white blouse had bloodstains on the back, the reason for which she explained. She had just taken on a kitten who would choose to launch himself at her back and dig his claws in, drawing blood. She drew me in and she seemed like the most honest person I had met in a long time. Neither of us had any other ulterior motive other than the want, or need, to find a suitably compatible partner. For life.

I had arranged to go and see my mum for a Sunday dinner later that evening but there must have been something about her as we chatted for about three hours before we decided to part. As I drove to mum's I felt a new direction in my life was about to take place.

We arranged to meet up again a few days later at an *all you can eat* Chinese restaurant, upon which I had to break the news that I already had a pre-booked holiday to Lindos. She was fine about it and we agreed to keep in contact after I returned. The next day she called me saying she had a free evening if I wanted to come over. It was the day before I was supposed to travel but I felt that it was worth pursuing, after all, this would be our *third date.*

The holiday was fraught with exchanges of text messages and I decided to go back and see her as soon as I returned, and by that I mean, I drove straight from Birmingham Airport to her flat and bypassed my mum's house and my own flat to see her.

Fast forward 20 years and we are still together and married for 18 of those years. Like all marriages, it has been difficult at times, but it is undoubtedly the best life decision I have ever made. To have that stability in a relationship is priceless.

I often get asked if I would do my time in Lindos again to which I will give a resounding "Yes", but that would only be if I could go back to those days when I was much younger and had fewer responsibilities. I wouldn't do it now as at this time in my life as I have too many other commitments, but could it be a retirement plan? No. I would want to enjoy Lindos again as I did before and nothing else.

I would never take away those years and would possibly do some things a little different but I really wouldn't change much. Twenty years of being with the same person teaches you that life doesn't always run smoothly and challenges are always around the corner. It's how you accept these challenges and deal with them that makes you a better person, unlike so many celebrity marriages who call it a day when their fame and recognition recedes and they realise they aren't on the front cover of *Hello!* every week.

We made a decision not to have children which I am thankful for.

It's probably quite important to realise that the ensuing rant is how I feel about the world today compared to the world I lived in when I was a Greek resident.

The only thing that hasn't changed for me is how I behave as a driver on English roads. If you drive in Greece, you just prepare yourself for every eventuality, whether it be an old Greek farmer escorting his herd of sheep or goats across a busy main road or just the fact that no one will give way to you as you would expect them to if you were on an English road. You become more tolerant of the idiocies on the road and you learn to tolerate bad drivers and wave them on their way with that Greek "tut" that the Greeks are famous for.

If you want to cut me up on a roundabout or overtake me in a 30mph speed limit I will just wave you on your way and hope that you crash into a ditch a few miles down the road. I'll be sure to report your fuckwit driving via my dashcam footage.

Everything else is just a one hundred per cent rant about the level of stupidity we have accepted as normal, so, if you're ready, let's read on. If not, this is the point you should put down this book or skip to Chapter Eleven so as not to hear the rantings of a grumpy old man. These are only opinions and observations and don't necessarily hold water.

When I finally left Lindos, it had changed

me for the better. Things that used to get me stressed out in the UK didn't matter anymore, and to all intents and purposes, I had become a Greek. The carefree way of life was now in my blood and I was prepared to continue that way.

In the last 20 years, however, the attitudes of the world have changed and I'm not sure I like what is happening. When I was a kid in the 70s, my brothers and my sister and I would be out all day, playing in dirt and chewing on grass that probably had dogs piss on it.

We would come home late, probably after dark, and our parents would never have been worried about where we were, even though we didn't have mobile phones to text them with. We would get straight into bed, without a bath and go to sleep in a room without central heating. In the summer it would be boiling hot and we would have crane-flies all over the walls, or daddy-long-legs as we used to call them. I remember mum on her hands and knees shovelling coal into the coal fire and lighting it which would supply us with our hot water. Looking back now it's no surprise that all of us kids shared the same bathwater as it wouldn't have been possible to shovel enough coal into a fire to heat up and run four separate baths. The thing is that I don't remember times being that hard as we grew up in a loving family, and we didn't know any different. This was just the only life that we knew, and none of our school friends lived in any better circumstances. Your status in life nowadays is determined by how much money your parents have, what brand of trainers you wear, and whether your current games console is up to date. What a shabby and worthless existence and a poor reflection of the society we have become.

Mum would prepare dinners, handling raw

meat without washing her hands and feed us every day, and at the end of all this, over 50 years later, we are still here to tell a tale. None of us ever caught salmonella or e-coli or any other bug because we were hard kids and our bodies were strong and healthy.

Someone decided that our homes weren't clean enough and so we now buy antibacterial products and scrub our homes and all of its surfaces clinically clean but nobody failed to spot that the more you sanitise, the more you give bacteria a cleaner surface to breed from.

This is the reason why we are experiencing a global pandemic as I write this. 40 years ago, our bodies were well prepared to give the nasty bacteria a monumental *fuck off and do one* but now we are inviting them into our homes and it seems they have become squatters with bacterial and civil rights. We seem unable to step outside the clinical environment of our homes without contracting some sort of illness.

I'm not sure whether I have become a grumpy old man or whether being back in the UK for the last twenty years or so has undone all the hard work that my time in Lindos did.

As a race, we have become unable to think for ourselves. We get told how we should prepare ourselves for heatwaves, but we are happy to take a holiday abroad where the temperatures in some foreign climates make our heatwaves seem like a mild spring.

We get told how to prepare ourselves for severe winters but we don't get the sort of winters we had when I was a child when we had a foot of snow on the ground but the milk float would still get our daily deliveries to us as if it were a normal day. If we get more than an inch of snow on the ground the country grinds to a halt and people stay at home for the day, most probably because they are malingerers who will use any excuse for a day off work.

We get warned on the news about flashing images and scenes that we may find upsetting and we get warned about TV programmes that contain language that some viewers might find offensive.

We get told how we should limit our alcohol intake, but if we all followed those guidelines there wouldn't be a pub in the country that could afford to stay open.

We are told we shouldn't smoke and we probably shouldn't, but many people smoke for most of their lives, in moderation, and live into their eighties and nineties, and others who choose not to smoke, die well before their time as they have inherited a mutant gene.

Life is a lottery. You can be the fittest and healthiest person you can aspire to be but you can get crushed by a lorry turning left as you pass in their blind spot on your bike, as cruel as that sounds.

It seems as though we need our hands holding through every step of our lives and I don't understand why or how this happened.

Having lost three members of my family well before their time I learned to accept that every day you stay on this earth is a bonus and nothing is guaranteed. You can't plan your future because you will never know what will happen from the time you wake up to the time you will go to bed. Most of us will make it through the day, but some of us won't.

We get told what foods we should and shouldn't eat but in reality, you should be able to eat anything you want. You can have a Maccy D's or a KFC every now and again and God knows there's nothing better than a kebab when you've been out on the drink for an evening but as long as you balance your diet nothing is too harmful. Eat red meat, have a bacon sandwich, take on some trans-fatty acids, but just mix it in with some vegetables, fruit, pasta and salad every now and again. Everything is ok for you in moderation.

It hardly surprises me that so many children are born with rare genetic disorders and it's because they have inherited the chemicals ingested by their parents with lazy diets who choose to buy pre-prepared meals from supermarkets that are loaded with preservatives and E numbers.

When I was at school I only really recall one or two of my classmates that was overweight or was a "speccy twat" or "four-eyes" as we would have probably renamed him. Or her.

We were all high functioning individuals

with varying levels of intellect and the promise to do well in life or just to fill the menial tasks that make the world go round. The clever kids were clever and the thick kids were thick. That was just the way the world worked and those who were clever went on to have professional careers and those who were a bit thick did other jobs that weren't so mentally challenging. We need bin collectors, supermarket shelf stackers, and people who dig holes in roads and lean on their shovels but we also need doctors, nurses, lawyers, skilled trades, civil engineers and market traders. We need entrepreneurs who can invent the next game-changing contraption but you shouldn't be made to feel any less worthy if you haven't got the mental agility to step up to the plate. We respect any job you do but the fact that only you can do that job shouldn't make you less of a person in society. We need to stop trying to promote people to levels of competence they will never achieve and accept them for who they are.

I hate Twitter and just about every form of Social Media in existence. I'm not interested in the benign illiterate opinions of a footballer or a TV reality star and I don't understand the mentality of normal people who see the need to follow every waking hour of these so-called celebrities.

I hate reality TV. I hate TV talent shows that make global sensations out of people with no talent other than the fact just about anyone will download their songs via iTunes and make them shitloads of money. I hate bloggers and Vloggers and YouTubers and people who make TikTok videos and that is purely because there is a section of society that doesn't know what a real job is anymore.

I'll applaud you but you've never done a proper days work in your life and you've never experienced the hardship of digging a cesspit in Lindos, or you've never left the comfort of your centrally heated home and got out of bed at 5 am to drive to work for two hours before putting in a days work and then driving home again. I hate you because if I was a little wiser I would have followed your incentives, but I didn't have your opportunities.

And I hate hipster beards as well. Why would any self-respecting young man make himself look thirty years older?

I get angry with the way the world is changing. Freedom of speech has been curtailed and people get offended by just about anything, whether it be posted online or spoken publicly. I would say it's a trait of the millennial generation but it seems that things we used to laugh at years ago without retribution are now considered offensive.

I would suggest it's a sign of the times but it seems that this conformity to be offended by things we used to laugh at decades ago has been adopted by people of my own age, just because they are scared of being labelled as racist or xenophobic.

Social media is completely responsible for this and while the idea of getting back in touch with old school friends was incepted by Friends Reunited, it was completely ruined when Facebook bought them out and turned it into a faceless medium in which the great unwashed of society could hammer out insults and opinions behind the security of their keyboards and fake email addresses. How ironic. An internet site designed to connect people has achieved exactly the opposite and driven them further apart.

Friends Reunited was started by a husband and wife team in a spare room in their house and, if Mark Zuckerburg offered you squillions of pounds to inherit your platform well….. Why wouldn't you?

The best possible advance in online technology is that if you misbehave online, you can be traced, via your IP address and you will do time at Her Majesty's Pleasure. Who knew? Just don't drop the soap in the shower. As I write this, we hear that those who made racist Tweets after England's Euro final defeat are about to be *sentenced*. Be careful what you write online is the best advice I can give, and this all comes from someone who used to write the most vitriolic X Factor Blogs…. but they were all in good humour, Your Honour.

The world is changing. Global warming and climate change is a real problem.

That will happen whether we like it or not and while I realise we have a responsibility to slow the process down we are small fishes in a very large pond.

We can make a difference but it will be small compared to what is happening elsewhere on the globe.

The population of New York State alone is currently over 20 million. This is only a third of the UK population. Can you even begin to imagine this? The entire population of this New York State makes up a third of the population of the UK, and it's all concentrated in one area instead of being spread across an entire country. So for every fat lazy American who drives to the shops instead of walking, or for every fat lazy American who gorges on a diet or red meat and burgers, or for every mentally unstable American who runs riot with a gun every now and again all that gunsmoke and cordite is doing more damage to our environment that a simple patio heater or a diesel engine. Now multiply that by the amount of states in America and the population of the USA and the population of China. Just take a minute to think about that one more time.

We know that the Americans and the Chinese are the biggest contributors to greenhouse gases and the combined population of these two countries is 1.75 billion so it makes our 68 million look a bit pathetic. So the next time Mrs Liberal/ Green Party starts to think about booking a holiday in a wet field in a tent with her hipster husband and two non-binary children because she's afraid of the damage a plane trip might do, perhaps the best advice would be not to worry. That plane will be taking off anyway so why not jump on board and get your arse over to Lindos, as it might even put a smile on your face for once although I'm not sure there are any vegan restaurants there just yet.

Thank you for reading my story and my end rant.

C hapter Eleven
Family Values

Brother Martin would finally succumb to his drug problems and pass away in 1999. He never really overcame his addictions and died after an overdose of Methadone which had been given to him by one of his like-minded *friends.* He was experimental to the very end.

Two years later, Dad suffered his first stroke, followed by another two. He passed away in 2006, surrounded by his family.

At the time, Mum was fit and healthy. We just thought she would go on forever. Just a year later, she was diagnosed with a brain tumour after a minor trans ischaemic attack. She fought it long and hard for three

years with debilitating bouts of chemo-
therapy and radiotherapy. We made the
difficult decision to put her into a final care
home, knowing that she probably wouldn't
have long. For God's sake, she was only in
her mid sixties. Sometimes in life, you wish
you could just roll back the years and try to
do something different that would change
a course of events. I did my best to come
and see her at weekends after working
away from home all week but I could see
her deterioration every time.

On the night we thought she would pass,
we were all present, expecting to say our
goodbyes, but she held out. I went home,
as did my brother, but Sue stayed the night.
She held mums hand as she passed away in
the morning and told her to go and be with
dad and Martin. I regret not being there but
I'm glad that she didn't die alone. She died
on 31st August 2010, so when the rest of
the world is remembering Princess Diana,

I am remembering someone whom I actually knew and loved.

I don't think about Mum every day of my life, or Dad, or even Martin, but every now and again, either one or all of them will feature in my dreams. I see it as a sign that they aren't gone forever and there is a time for a reunion.

Do I believe in the afterlife? Of course not. When you're gone, you are gone and nothing can bring you back. You can't be reincarnated as a cat or anything else, but if they are waiting up there for the rest of us to join them, then I'll be sure to let them know that we can all be a family again if I'm the next on the list.

In a way, I feel glad that my parents aren't around to witness the shit show that the world has become, but, by juxtaposition, they would have loved to have seen how we have all grown up and made successes of our lives and to have seen their grandchildren blossom into young adults.

But then again they were both born in the 40s when the world was a poorer place and they both grew up in relative poverty, so it would have only been a natural progression for the world to get better, although they wouldn't have known this at the time. I feel that they, and the generation before them, paved the way to make the world a better place but subsequent generations are reversing this process and undoing all the hard work. I feel thankful, in some small way, that we don't have offspring to inherit an unknown world.

Chapter Twelve

The Last Words

I dedicate this book to the following people, in no particular order. These are people that I met in my life in Lindos that made an impression on me for whatever reason. If I didn't mention you it's because this book was about me and not you, but I remember you fondly anyway.

The *ghosts* have been italicised.

My wife Paula, who has managed to stay with me for twenty years and has managed to tolerate me and all my traits.

Mum and Dad, brother Bob and sister Sue, and brother *Martin. Cliff*, Rena and Natalie.

Bob Penny. *Twink.* Mark, Michelle, and *Pete Madely, Lee Balmer,* Ellie and Phil. Superjock. Robbo and Lindos' longest standing DJ Yannis Kapetanis. And Manolis Anastiadtis. Jack, Sam, and all your extended family, especially Marianthi and *Apostolis.* Carl, Lee and Martin, the one and only and still unique Lost Boys. Phil and Barbara. Tracy and Judith, The Rainbird Girls. The Alphabet Street Girls, and the legendary Rudy. Ski J. John and Mark. Sarah, Ruthie, Gill and *Basil. Captain and Dimitris Takis.* Evripides and Kiki. Dimitris Savaidais and Nikos – my competition to the right, and all the other sunbed boys on the beach. The Jody's Flat crew. Mike and *Mary* Stadiatis. Nikos Psaros. Chrissie. Bob. Carolyn. Jörg and Jennie (thanks for coming that night). Hellas Jack, Eftichia, Kyriakos and Giorgos. Enigma Mikhalis and Sotiris. Vassilis. Tracey and Louise, my Lindos Gardens compatriots. Rachel.

And anyone else who knew me.

Efkharisto. And Kalinichta.
Thank you. And Goodnight.

Printed in Great Britain
by Amazon